How To Open
The Heart

How To Open The Heart

*An Incredible Journey Into Vulnerability,
Empathy, And The Transformation Of
Consciousness*

Miles Olsen

The events and conversations in this book have been set down to the best of the author's ability, although some names and details have been changed to protect the privacy of individuals.

First paperback edition November 2020

ISBN 978-1-7774652-0-9 (paperback)

milesolsen.com

Contents

How To Open The Heart

Chapter One

When I was thirteen years old, nearly every day after I got home from school there was a golden hour of celebration. With just my younger brother Lonnie and I around the house, I could fully let go and be myself. There were no parents, teachers or other adults present to kill the fun, and no friends, peers or classmates to feel uncool or self-conscious around.

On the surface, I doubt it would have appeared as though anything remarkable was taking place during these brief moments of my afternoon. For the most part, I would just make snacks, listen to music or watch TV. But at a deeper level, I was breathing easy, relaxing and feeling calm for the first time that day. This was a precious window in which I could feel a sense of naturalness and drop my guard.

Then, around the same time every afternoon, the party would come to an abrupt end. My father's car would roll up the driveway, and as soon as I heard the growl of its engine outside or the crash of its driver's side door slamming shut, a pang of fear would shoot through my body. In a state of panic, I would rush to put away whatever it was I had been doing, clean up after myself and try to get to my bedroom before my father got into the house and we crossed paths.

When he got home from work, my dad's mood was pretty predictable: He would be fuming with frustration and exuding an intense, brooding rage that I could feel from a distance. As he made his way into the house, he would often make loud, angry comments regarding some crumbs left on the counter, or any other minor annoyance.

My father was not physically violent towards us, but his energy itself felt violent. Though it only struck out through words and feelings, it was a powerful force. My body would seize up as though it were bracing for impact in his presence, and on an emotional or energetic level, there were many blows to absorb, duck and dive from.

As a thirteen year old, I couldn't understand why he carried this simmering, seething anger around all the time. All I knew was that I felt perpetually unwelcome in his home because of it, and longed for the day when I could be as far as humanly possible from such an oppressive and harsh emotional landscape.

By my mid-twenties, it had been many years since I'd left my childhood home. During that time, I had made some pretty extreme life choices in order to separate myself from my family's dysfunctional dynamics and patterns: I was living off the grid as part of a small, close-knit, rugged backwoods homestead. This was a significant departure from my relatively ordinary, suburban Canadian upbringing. By going in such an alternative direction, I'd attempted to create an entirely different experience and turn away from the things I disliked about the world I grew up in. You can imagine how annoying it was, then, when one of the people living at the homestead turned out to be a new embodiment of all the brooding anger and frustration I'd dreamed of finding refuge from throughout my childhood and youth.

Most of the time, this person was extremely magnetic, playful, friendly and charismatic. He was often the life of the party, and was deeply appreciated and respected by everyone in our little community. But even at the best of times, there was another side to him, an undercurrent of angst and frustration that was unpredictable, untamed and frightening. It could easily be triggered and seize him at any moment, and when that happened, he could be extremely cold and harsh, slicing through people with his cruel words and closed-hearted, contemptuous tone. Even though this cold, angry part of him was usually dormant, it sometimes felt as though it coloured the whole atmosphere of our shared living environment. A few of my housemates would habitually tiptoe around him, fearing his volatility.

The most difficult part of this situation, however, was that the person I am describing was actually me. I was that guy, carrying the brooding anger my friends tiptoed around. And I had absolutely no idea that this was the case. My self-image and the more complex, objective reality of who I actually was (which everyone outside of me could clearly see), did not match. As far as I was concerned, I was the kindest, most sensitive guy in the world. My friends, however, would have told a slightly different story, one that was a bit more nuanced and less flattering.

Occasionally, my friends would hint at this uncomfortable reality by saying something out of annoyance or complete exasperation with me. One of them might reach a breaking point and ask: "Miles, why are you always so angry? It's scary to be around!" In response I would generally get angrier than I already was, my energy becoming tense, my voice getting louder and deeper, and I would proceed to heatedly explain that I wasn't angry at all, they were just insecure or delusional. Probably both.

It was always easy to brush off the little nudges my friends dropped for me ("Miles, you can be really intimidating to be around," or "Miles, I feel like I wouldn't want to say the wrong thing around you!" etc). I just assumed they were weak and jealous of my natural strength and confidence. It was them with the problem, not me, I assured myself.

As life unfolded, however, a series of events conspired to make me second guess my certainty on this matter.

One winter evening at the homestead, a group of us were crammed into our communal cabin for dinner, talking amongst ourselves and having a good time. Over the course of the evening, I'd been engaging in an ongoing joke with my fellow homesteaders about a Canadian politician named Jack Layton.

Canada was in the midst of a national election, and Jack Layton was running to lead the country as Prime Minister. Although I was generally quite disconnected from and disinterested in politics at the time, there was a charm, authenticity, and charisma to Jack Layton that captured my attention. Half-jokingly, I was trying to persuade my friends to vote for him, acting as an unofficial campaigner for Mr. Layton. Because this kind of political engagement was so out of character for me, everyone thought I was being funny and sarcastic, which to a certain extent I was. I liked Jack Layton, but didn't really take any of this very seriously, although it was fun to play around as though I did.

One of my friends jokingly took the position of slandering and defaming Mr. Layton, which was a sarcastic and fun counterpoint to my stance. As the night wore on, however, my friend's slander and character assassinations grew harsher, and my threshold for sarcasm began to wear through. Aware that the joke wasn't feeling funny anymore, I asked her a few times to please stop with the jabs against Jack Layton, saying that it was getting old. I could feel a raw nerve in me being prodded with each of her jokes, but she was having too much fun, and couldn't help but continue enjoying herself.

Eventually, after one too many distasteful words were uttered against Jack Layton, the raw nerve in me got fully irritated and, like a child whose sibling has taunted them one too many times, I exploded. Standing up, fuming with anger, I bellowed through the full room that anyone who didn't like Jack Layton could go to the far side of the cabin, and all those that did like him could come to my side.

The room completely froze in silence, and everyone stared at me as though I'd just erupted into a hateful tirade. I had no idea what the big deal was - I'd just found a solution to this annoying problem of my friend bothering me, and announced it with a little force.

After a few moments of excruciating silence, I decided to excuse myself and went outside to take a breath of fresh air. When I returned to the cabin a couple of minutes later, I found a rather surprising event unfolding: My friends had arranged themselves into a single row of chairs against one wall of the cabin, each of them facing towards the centre of the room. Across from them, in the middle of the space, was a single empty chair. They told me to take a seat in it. I looked at them sitting in a row facing me, then I looked at the little lone chair, and realized that I was being put on some kind of trial.

I took my seat, and my housemates proceeded to tell me how unacceptable my outburst had been, and how it was just the latest eruption in a chronic pattern of mine. One after another, they each took turns explaining how out of line and hurtful my behaviour was, as I sat and burned in shame. Like a scene from a wilderness survival gameshow, my peers aired their grievances with an emotional charge in the reddish flickering glow of candlelight, letting me know that I had been the bad contestant. And although I wasn't exactly being voted out of the group, it pretty much felt like it. I don't clearly remember any of what they said once I took my place in that hot seat, except that I'd been borderline abusive and hurt my friend's feelings, which made absolutely no sense to me. I felt I had done nothing wrong, that I'd just been acting in self-defence, and wondered how everyone couldn't clearly see that I was the victim in this situation. It was obvious to me that I'd simply been pushed to the edge by my friend's sarcastic remarks, and then pushed back. Everyone else, however, felt that I had been wildly aggressive and out of line.

As my friends vented their outrage at me, I kept on looking at certain individuals, wondering when they were going to stick up for me and say something to balance things out, waiting for someone to have my back. When that didn't happen, it felt as though a part of me simply crumpled up and shut down. I felt like I was being hit over the head with shame and rejection. I felt unwelcome in my own home, and had an immediate, overwhelming impulse to move as far away from these people as possible, as quickly as I could. My time in that seat of shame wasn't long, but it burned deeply.

After hearing what everyone had to say, and being as diplomatic and restrained in my response as possible, I hobbled off to my own little cabin for the night. Walking alone in the dark, rainy forest, I felt confused, sad, and annoyed that everyone I lived with was apparently insecure, jealous, and caught up in some strange collective delusion. I let nothing they had said sink in. And, to be fair, the way that it had been delivered wasn't the most mature or graceful. Singling an individual out and shaming them collectively in an emotionally heated way is often not the smoothest form of communication or conflict resolution. Still, however messy that impromptu trial had been, the consensus amongst my peers about my behaviour was a curious thing. Even in the throes of

Chapter One

my shame, sadness and anger, at the very back of my mind I couldn't help but wonder about that.

A few days later, the events of that night felt like a distant memory when my friend Daniel and I set out on a short trip together. We were headed to visit a friend in the city, about a three-hour drive from where we lived, and had decided to hitchhike there. This was something we were both accustomed to and comfortable with from years of travel.

We arrived early in the morning at a highway on-ramp that marked the departure point for our journey. After a few minutes of waiting on the roadside, we decided that it would be wise for us to split up and hitchhike separately. One scruffy adult male trying to get picked up on the side of a road was difficult enough to sell, the two of us together were a bit much. And so Daniel chose to walk a ways down the road, leaving me alone at the on-ramp. This put me at an advantage for getting a ride sooner, as I would be seen by passing cars before Daniel was. In addition to that, I was situated along a stretch of road where those cars would be driving at a slower speed and could pull over more easily and safely if they wanted to. Daniel was content to walk further along the highway and take a less preferable position, so we wished each other good luck before he headed down the road and eventually out of sight.

After waiting for what felt like hours, I finally got a ride with a young man who drove only a short distance before he had to turn off the highway and drop me off. Feeling disappointed, I resumed my post on the roadside and waited for over an hour before getting picked up again. A demoralizing pattern of long waits and short rides repeated itself half a dozen times before I eventually reached the outskirts of the city late in the evening. When I finally made it to my destination, I was completely exhausted, and to my surprise, Daniel had already been there for quite some time, enjoying himself and relaxing.

Apparently he'd made quick progress, getting picked up almost immediately by a woman who went out of her way to drive him right to his destination. After Daniel asked me how my trip was, he was eager to share a passing comment the woman had made during their drive: According to her, there had been another guy hitchhiking on the road immediately before she saw Daniel. She explained that she would have happily picked this other guy (me) up, but he looked "*really angry*". When she saw Daniel, however, she immediately felt that he looked kind and friendly, so didn't think twice about pulling over to offer him a ride.

Daniel thought this was very funny - I was annoyed and perplexed by it. I explained to him that I hadn't been angry at all, and wondered what this woman had been talking about? I figured she must be yet another crazy person projecting her insecurities onto me, just like everyone had done a few nights earlier at the cabin. I was somewhat aware, however, that this theory became a bit tenuous when a complete stranger's observations were at play. Still, I sincerely had not felt angry, and so whatever this lady thought she had seen in me was baffling.

As I got worked up defending myself against this unknown woman's perception of me, Daniel's only response was to say: "I'm just telling you what she told me."

During our trip to the city, I was visiting the downtown library and bumped into an acquaintance named David Jonas. David was a flamboyant character that had the appearance of a classic, quintessential hippie. He donned a massive beard, long sun-bleached hair, was often barefoot, wore loose-fitting clothes, and sometimes carried a sign with a philosophical or protest statement scrawled on it. The only one of these signs I remember clearly stated 'Pride Is Sin' in bold writing. I was never close to David, and had rarely ever spoken with him, but on this afternoon we exchanged a warm hello, after which he enthusiastically recounted a dream he'd recently had. I played a prominent role in this dream, and he felt that I needed to hear about it.

In David's dream, I was a vampire. Actually, I was a leader of a group of vampires, and David was tracking me down to kill me. At the end of the dream, after some drama and difficulty, David finally overpowered me and thrust a wooden stake into my chest and through my heart, violently ending my reign of terror.

"It's something you might want to think about," David said, after vividly describing his dream.

I didn't understand what he meant by this, so asked him to explain.

"You being a vampire," he replied. "That's something you might want to seriously think about. Are you aware of that part of yourself?"

I was sincerely confused, and pretty convinced David was insane. His tone, however, still strikes me when I remember this interaction - David seemed genuinely caring and concerned. It was as though he felt that he had a responsibility to share this information (his insight into my vampiric nature) with me, and there was a deep compassion, tenderness, and an almost paternal feeling to the way in which he delivered it. It was as though he just really wanted to help a vampire see the light.

I left our interaction shaking my head. David, with his wild appearance and tattered, 'Pride Is Sin' sign, was easy to dismiss. But something about his dream stuck with me. That, as well as the woman who decided not to pick me up, the painful backwoods trial I'd been put on by my peers, and the ongoing remarks from friends about my harshness or scariness, felt unsettling. Although I was pretty sure all of their perspectives were nonsense, an uncertainty was beginning to grow in the back of my mind as information continued coming at me from various directions. A tiny gap in my armour was forming, and during quiet moments alone, in a distant corner of myself, I began to wrestle with the question that all philosophers and truth-seekers across the ages have grappled with: *Am I actually an asshole?*

Chapter Two

Around the same time that all of the events I just recounted occurred, I met a man named Kevin, who seemed almost heaven-sent to answer the big question I was beginning to wrestle with. Kevin was introduced to me by Daniel, my closest friend and fellow homesteader. Daniel and I had lived together in the woods for many years, and had been friends since I was about thirteen years old. At this point in time, Daniel had decided to leave our homestead and move back into town, as his interest in backwoods living had waned and other passions were calling him. He rented a room in an old, two-bedroom house in a quiet neighbourhood that was shared with one other tenant. That other tenant was Kevin, a man who quickly turned out to be a very gifted and fascinating individual.

Shortly after moving in, Daniel told me that his new roommate was some kind of clairvoyant or psychic that could "feel absolutely everything going on inside of people." Because of this, living with him was like being emotionally naked at all times. When Daniel spoke, Kevin could feel if something wasn't true or if something was being withheld, and he could feel what Daniel's energy and emotions were saying nonverbally. When Daniel said something that didn't feel true to Kevin, he would call Daniel out on the discrepancy between what was being spoken out loud, and the energy that was present beneath the words. Usually, Daniel would end up owning his lack of honesty or authenticity, though sometimes only after a lengthy argument which resulted in him being completely exposed.

Hearing these things about Kevin before ever seeing him, I expected him to be wearing baggy hemp pants, adorned with crystal necklaces and bracelets, his hair tied back into a neat ponytail or sculpted into dreadlocks. I also expected the dignified, calm, and righteous ambience of a person who strongly identifies as spiritually elevated. I was quite surprised to discover upon meeting him, however, that his appearance and countenance were completely plain and unassuming. Aside from Kevin's imposing height and stature (he stood six foot five inches tall, with a broad, sturdy frame), he had the image and ambience that I'd expect more from a geeky software developer than an esoteric savant. He dressed in blue jeans, a t-shirt and sneakers, had a shaved head, and fit basically none of the tropes or superficial stereotypes I'd come to expect from a hippy or spiritual individual.

I was arriving to visit Daniel the first time Kevin and I crossed paths. This encounter was very brief, as Kevin was leaving while I walked up the front steps. He very quietly said hello while he wheeled his bicycle past me. My initial impression was simply that he seemed pretty nice, and strangely normal. He didn't look like a clairvoyant or overtly spiritual person at all. This only made me more curious to find out about his rumoured gifts and abilities.

Apparently, Kevin's first impression of me wasn't quite so open or curious. Years after we initially met, he told me that from our first encounter, he knew immediately that he didn't like me at all. He thought I was an arrogant, closed-hearted, toxic alpha male. Not a great first impression, but somehow our story didn't end there.

Because Daniel and I were best friends, I ended up visiting his new home quite a bit, and through this association I found myself witnessing Kevin's gifts in action regularly and becoming quite intrigued by them. The most striking example of Kevin's abilities during my initial visits occurred when I began writing a little booklet about living in the woods. I intended to put together some writing I'd been doing over the previous couple of years, adding some new work and printing off a small, self-made project to share with friends and anyone else interested in my thoughts and experiences. It wasn't anything too audacious, and certainly nothing too professional, though I was very passionate about this little creative endeavour.

One afternoon, I was visiting Kevin and Daniel when I began to tell them about this new project. As I described a rough idea of what I was envisioning, Kevin suddenly stood up and interrupted me mid-sentence, shouting: "Miles, this is amazing! You've got white light pouring through your head right now! Who are you getting to publish your book? Which publisher?"

I liked the idea that I had white light pouring through my head while speaking about this booklet, but I had no idea what Kevin was talking about regarding a publisher. I informed him that I was going to publish the booklet myself, by going to a local print shop or library, printing it out and stapling it together. It was a humble DIY project, nothing more, nothing less.

Kevin shook his head, insisting that I wasn't seeing what he was seeing, and somewhat of an argument ensued.

"Miles, nothing that you just said grounded," he explained. "That's not what's happening here. You've got white light pouring through your head, and this book - and it is a book, not a booklet or whatever you said - is going to be published by the first publisher you contact. That is one hundred percent guaranteed!"

Again, I tried to explain to Kevin that none of what he was saying made any sense - I was completely unknown, I lived in the woods and didn't even have a phone or electricity. Nobody was going to be publishing anything I wrote any time soon.

He replied: "Miles, I am going to say this once again: You have white light pouring through your head. Believe me when I tell you that you will get this book published by the first publisher you contact. I guarantee it. The energy is so clear here that it's basically already a done deal. This book is already published, you just have to go through a few simple motions in order for things to fall into place so it can be realized. I one hundred percent guarantee everything I'm feeling is real. The energy is as clear as it gets."

I continued to resist Kevin's lofty prediction, which only seemed to make him more emphatic, until I realized this was somewhat of a ridiculous argument for me to make. Since his prediction was so positive and he was so confident with it, I decided it would be best to simply test his 'guarantee' (a word he kept on repeating with great emphasis) - I would do whatever people do when they want to get a book published, and see if he was right. Of course I had no idea what that might entail.

Kevin offered some guidance here, first asking me to take a seat across from him in his living room. Once we were seated comfortably, he told me to close my eyes and look for the ideal publisher in my mind. I wasn't entirely sure what he was wanting me to do with that suggestion, but when I closed my eyes, relaxed, and focused for a few moments, the logo of a publisher immediately came into my mind's eye.

"Did you find them yet?" He asked.

"I think so, one came to my mind."

"Perfect, you've got it. Now go google how to make a submission to them, and you're off to the races! It shouldn't take long at all for you to have a contract signed with them for your book."

I left this interaction feeling a mixture of confusion and excitement. If what Kevin was saying was true, it was great news. It seemed totally implausible and absurd, but I had nothing to lose by trying. And, by going along with his suggestion, I would find out very quickly if he was totally off base or not. With this in mind, I went ahead and researched how to make a proper book submission to the publisher that had popped into my awareness in Kevin's living room. Over the following week, I wrote and assembled all of the requisite materials for this, and as soon as that was done, I sent a proposal via email for what was now my book to the submissions department of that publisher. Then I waited with bated breath to see what would happen.

I did not have to wait long. It was only a few hours before I received an enthusiastic response from an editor, saying that she really liked what I'd written and would like to see more material. Within weeks I found myself negotiating and signing a contract with this publisher for my first book. This was, as had been predicted, the first publisher I contacted.

Kevin had been right. Somehow he'd seen or felt everything clearly. And to make things even more interesting, he had absolutely no idea if I could write, what I was going to be writing about, or who I really was, and yet he somehow had a complete knowingness that this would happen in the way he foresaw. It also may be worth mentioning that a completely unknown writer, with no following or reputation of any kind, getting published by the first publisher they contact is almost unheard of. To me it seemed unreal.

Kevin, however, was completely unsurprised when he heard the news that I had gotten a book deal. "This was as clear as it gets," he said, assuring me there was no part of him that had questioned the energy he felt even in the slightest. "This is just what I do," he explained. "I can feel your energy incredibly clearly, and I know how it will interact with the world - I know what it will bring into your life or push out of it. In this case, getting a book deal was a certainty before you even knew what you were doing. It was blatantly obvious."

This was just one of countless similar experiences that occurred during the first summer I spent visiting Kevin and Daniel's home. As a result of such incidents, I found myself stopping by their place more and more often. Kevin's ability to see, sense, and feel the energy of an individual was incredibly sophisticated, but even more captivating was how he shared everything he saw: Passionately and with absolutely no filter.

With my book, he aggressively stepped in to share a bigger vision that he felt I needed to hear about, regardless of the fact that I was a stranger who he didn't particularly like at the time. I soon realized that this was how he operated under all circumstances. He functioned as a big, clear voice for whatever energy he felt and saw in the moment. He was always studying the deeper dimensions of reality, aware of currents of energy and emotion that most others are inured to, and passionately, emphatically calling everyone's attention to them.

Kevin did not call himself a psychic, and would probably dislike that I'm even bringing that word up in relation to him. He said that he was simply empathic - able to feel and see the energy and emotion of others acutely. He also described himself as being more aware of his connection to 'truth' than most others. In practical terms, this meant that when someone was speaking and they made a statement that was authentic to their very core ('in truth'), he could feel the quality of their energy as a result. Such energy felt light, life-giving, natural and strong. It was grounded and had the stable, authentic feeling of truth. This was not an abstract concept of truth, but an actual energy of authenticity and alignment. In the case of my book, when I spoke about it Kevin felt pure white light pouring through me, and that energy got him excited about the life of a guy he otherwise felt was an arrogant, obnoxious alpha male he'd rather didn't drop by his house at all. The book was in truth for me, and Kevin could feel that.

Conversely, when someone made a statement that wasn't true, that was inauthentic or out of alignment with their real self, Kevin felt what that did to their energy. He could feel their energy twisting and contorting into something forced and unnatural, disconnecting, pretending, lying, hiding and cheating. It was not grounded, and didn't feel like truth. He felt this energy in others so acutely that just as he got excited about my book, he would get sickened or upset by extremely disjointed energy (someone who was seriously out of alignment with their truth).

To me, Kevin seemed like a magician, capable of reading an individual and, in some ways, knowing them much better than they even knew themselves (he didn't have their self-deception or wounds blocking his view, after all). Kevin claimed that everyone was capable of this level of perception, that it wasn't anything esoteric or spiritual at all, it was just being connected to reality.

In addition to his emotional and energetic awareness, Kevin was also capable of seeing how an individual's energy would ripple into their world and create their present or future reality. That was how he could 'guarantee' my book deal, among other things.

The second very memorable demonstration of Kevin's empathic abilities came around the same time as the book experience I just recounted. Where the book and his predictions around it were exciting and joyful to experience, this situation was a little more complex.

It wasn't long after meeting Kevin that I found myself in a state of desperation and heartbreak. I had fallen in love with a young woman, and after several months of dating, she announced she wanted to make the relationship open, to be polyamorous and avoid the pitfalls and limitations of monogamy.

Intellectually, I understood this and was open to it. I had seen signs that such a conversation might be coming from the beginning of our connection. On an emotional level, however, this situation felt completely devastating. I found myself in what is probably a fairly common dilemma: I didn't want to limit or restrain the natural will and desire of my lover. I could also intellectually see how monogamy might be inherently unnatural, nothing more than an outdated and oppressive tradition that I'd been conditioned into. But inside, I was dying. My mind was fully open, but my heart felt like it was being mercilessly bludgeoned at the mere thought of being in an open relationship with this woman. No part of me wanted to be with other people, and having my lover be with other men felt like a form of intense emotional torture. But I questioned my feelings. Was I just an oppressive male, conditioned into an old, patriarchal pattern of owning a woman's body? Was that why I felt so bad, because I hadn't yet outgrown this possessive type of relationship? I couldn't square the two opposing forces in me: My intellectual understanding and openness, and the unrelenting emotional storm in me that couldn't care less about any rationalization whatsoever.

After weeks of agonizing over this situation, I wondered if Kevin, who at this point was still more or less a stranger to me, might have some insights. If he could read my energy, he could finally confirm whether or not I was in fact a toxic male oppressor that simply couldn't get over himself. I suspected I was, and it would be a relief for someone to finally just give it to me straight.

I arrived on his doorstep early one morning and asked if he would be open to helping me with something. He graciously invited me in and asked me to take a seat in a yellow chair positioned at one end of his large, unfurnished living room. At the other end of the room was another identical yellow chair where he took a seat. Facing one another from opposite sides of the room, I began to share my dilemma.

There was an electricity and an intensity in the room with Kevin that no words can accurately capture. His presence was so strong, focused, penetrating and graceful that nothing felt normal. It felt almost like we were in an altered state - things seemed more lucid, hairs stood on end and the walls seemed to crackle in the silence of this charged atmosphere.

I went into detail explaining everything going on in my relationship, but Kevin stopped me about halfway through my sharing, saying he already had enough information. With his eyes closed, he sat in silence for a minute or two, occasionally nodding and whispering something quietly to himself, before launching into his response.

He shared that everything I was feeling (my emotional response of pain and devastation to this situation) was natural, sacred, and beautiful. My heart, according to him, felt like it was dying because it was in a situation that was wildly inconsistent with its needs and design.

"I'm actually impressed with what I'm seeing in you," he said. "I honestly didn't think your heart had this kind of maturity. All it wants, all you want, is to love in a very complete and full way, and to receive that back. There is nothing unclean whatsoever here, no manipulation or neediness. Just a heart that is ready to love in a certain way and isn't being met. It's absolutely beautiful."

He passionately validated and celebrated the kind of relationship my heart longed to experience, and I began sobbing uncontrollably. Kevin wasn't offering advice or motivation. He wasn't referencing a theory of relationship or psychology. It was as though he was actually seeing my heart, actually reaching into me and holding one of my deepest and most vulnerable places with a sincerity, understanding and nurturance I'd never felt before. He was having a direct conversation with a hurt and confused part of me, offering it unflinching love and support.

I'd never experienced anything like this, but the most surprising thing came after my tears were beginning to dry. Kevin's eyes closed again, and after a few subtle nods and hushed comments to himself, he announced that there was more to this story.

"Miles, I have good news and bad news. Which one do you want first?"

I thought about this for a moment, then asked for the good stuff.

"The good news is, you get the girl," he said. "The bad news is, it's not this one. This is most definitely not the girl for you. But that isn't actually bad news at all, because the one for you is going to feel much better, and she is basically already here!"

I was confused. It seemed like Kevin was breaking some kind of unspoken law by jumping to this conclusion and telling me what would happen down the road. By doing so it felt like he was interfering with my process. But more importantly, I was in love with my girlfriend. There was no way I was about to end my relationship with her, and now that I knew what my needs were, I only planned to share them openly and see how she responded.

Chapter Two

Kevin was already several steps ahead of me, though. "Miles," he said, with his eyes closed, "there are already five women waiting for you, I can see them all clearly right now! They are extremely close, and are literally waiting for you to simply become available so you can connect with one of them."

I had no idea what to think at this point. Part of me was admittedly intrigued by the notion of five mysterious women waiting for me at that moment, but I was still totally attached to my current relationship. After some back and forth, Kevin gave me a warning: He conceded that my girlfriend would try to meet my needs once I shared them with her, but that the relationship itself was fundamentally not in truth. He explained that this was what the entire situation I'd come to discuss with him was trying to show me - that there were some fundamental areas where my girlfriend and I simply didn't match. If I chose to learn the lesson now, he insisted that there was something significantly better waiting for me immediately. In fact, there were five specific people he distinctly felt waiting. If I chose to remain with my girlfriend, however, the same painful dynamic would inevitably resurface. The two of us could try and make it work, try to twist ourselves into fitting one another's needs, but he was absolutely certain that it would end badly no matter what. He was quite emphatic about this, saying that it would be a very grave mistake for me to carry on in my current relationship.

I left Kevin's house that day thinking that he was both one of the most impressive people I'd ever met, and that he was also maybe a little bit off. There was no question in my mind that I was going to stay with my girlfriend and try to make things work with her.

A couple of months after this initial warning from Kevin, I was still in the same relationship. And, as predicted, the suffering and drama did continue. Kevin had been correct that

21

my girlfriend would try to make things work when I owned my true feelings around polyamory, and it also seemed that regardless of our best efforts and intentions, our underlying issues and ongoing clashing wouldn't go away.

One afternoon I got home to the cabin I shared with my friends after a brief outing to find that a bear had ransacked the exterior of the place. Boxes of stored apples were knocked over, the ground was torn up, and piles of fresh bear dung were deposited on the doorstep, leaving no question as to who or what had made the mess.

This was notable because, after years of living in the woods, it was the one and only time that any wild animal had come and disturbed our home. Previously, it was as though there was some kind of force field around our cabin. It was actually quite bizarre, but despite storing all kinds of food on the porch regularly, no creature had ever been so bold as to come near the house and help themselves to it. My friends and I would jokingly refer to this as the result of some kind of spell we had cast or an agreement we had with the forest, and until this afternoon it had held in place across many years. I actually had a hard time processing that a bear really had broken this pattern, and now may become habituated to snacking at my cabin. The mess itself was annoying, but in the bigger picture it meant I would need to significantly change how I did things to prevent it from happening again.

The next time I saw Kevin, I mentioned this bear incident in passing and he immediately got excited, nearly shouting: "It's your girlfriend!" He was convinced that this event was related to my ongoing relationship drama, and that the bear violated my boundaries because that was what was happening in my love life - my boundaries were being crossed and trampled on by my girlfriend. Once again, I thought Kevin was a bit off and discounted his thoughts.

When I checked my messages immediately after our conversation, however, I noticed a new one from my girlfriend, letting me know that she planned to dress up as a bear for Halloween. I told Kevin about this and he shook his head.

"Miles, could it be any clearer?" he asked. "Do you need an angel to fly by with a banner that reads 'Your girlfriend is the bear,' or is this obvious enough? I'm actually quite serious right now. Please, listen to me. Things are going to get really bad if you don't change course immediately. I mean it. You will be physically harmed if you carry on in this relationship. It might come in the form of a car accident, or it might mean getting mauled by that bear. I don't know exactly how, but this will escalate if you don't make a change. I'm dead serious."

I knew Kevin wasn't joking, but there was still no way I was ready to extract myself from my relationship.

A few days later, I left my cabin early in the morning after a sleepless night. The previous day I'd learned that my girlfriend had spent some time with another young man at a party without telling me. They didn't sleep together, but as she reluctantly described their interaction, it was clear that they had engaged with each other in a way that violated the type of exclusive relationship we'd both committed to. The issue of exclusivity in our relationship had come up again, and once again I felt an overwhelming anguish being caught in the middle of it. The exact sensation was something like having a dagger lodged in my heart, slowly sinking and twisting in a raw wound.

After a restless night, I decided to visit Kevin and Daniel first thing in the morning. As I rode my bike down a steep hill towards their house in the depths of my emotion, a car waiting at a stop sign decided to hit the gas and lurch onto the road the moment I was crossing its path.

Suddenly everything turned slow motion, and I watched in shock as the front tire of my bike crashed into the bumper of this car. I was flung over the hood of the vehicle, flipping in the air and landing with a thud on the pavement downhill from it.

As I laid on the roadside and began to register what was happening, I realized that somehow, miraculously, I had no immediately apparent injuries. My bike was destroyed by the impact, but as I slowly got up from the pavement, my body appeared to be okay.

An old lady stepped out of the car, appearing to be just as shaken as me, and I proceeded to scream a long list of obscenities at her. It was a bizarre mistake she'd made, ploughing directly into me in broad daylight (apparently the sun had been in her eyes when she decided to pull onto the road), and I let myself rage at her in an unhinged, instinctive way (which I immediately regretted). After thoroughly venting at this poor old woman, I calmed down and asked her to drive me to Kevin and Daniel's, since my bike was no longer of any use.

When I arrived there and told Kevin what had just happened, his reaction was first one of concern that I was okay, quickly followed by a very serious, solemn warning.

"Miles, I don't know what to say. The next step here is you leaving the earth. I told you this would happen, that things would escalate, and believe me when I tell you that they will continue to. You have to understand what an escalation from getting seriously hit by a car means. It means game over. It means your life ends. I am dead serious Miles. If you carry on with this trajectory, this might be our last conversation."

I could feel Kevin's sincerity and concern, and given everything that had been happening, his pleas were beginning to get through. Although my intellect still wasn't fully on board with Kevin's whole view of reality as some kind of predictable reflection of an individual's energy or emotion, I finally decided that enough was enough, and reluctantly ended my relationship after this car accident. While I could clearly see and feel what wasn't working with my girlfriend, and knew our connection was a source of ongoing suffering, a part of me really didn't want to let her go, even with the possible threat of death now looming near.

Because I was still so attached to this relationship, breaking up was quite difficult. There was an initial sense of relief, and Kevin was very congratulatory, celebrating that I'd made what in his view was an extremely important and positive decision. It wasn't long, however, before a heavy cloud of sadness and despair settled over me. I'd formed such a strong bond with my now ex, that stepping away from her felt torturous. After a week or so of separation, it felt as though every cell in my body just wanted to go back to her. I slid into a kind of lovesick panic, convinced that I'd made the wrong decision, that this was all a tragic error and I needed to immediately reconnect with, and embrace, my star-crossed lover.

When I showed up at Kevin's doorstep in this state, his advice was clear: "You've gone temporarily insane, Miles. Nothing you're thinking or believing right now makes any sense whatsoever. You're an addict who has had his substance of choice taken away, and you've lost your mind while you go through withdrawals. It's that simple. I'd try to help you process your emotions and show you how to work with some of what you're feeling right now, but honestly, your energy is too crazy for any of that at the moment. You don't actually feel amenable to such an intervention. So what I'd suggest is that you go home to your cabin, and don't do anything for a few days. Don't leave. Don't make any decisions. Just breathe, make food, chop wood, do whatever you do with yourself up there. But do not make any decisions about anything meaningful until this has settled. And absolutely do not contact your ex. That would be a disaster."

Kevin paused and closed his eyes to examine something. "One thing that I actually would recommend you do," he continued, "is disconnect your energy from her. You two are still completely connected energetically, in a way that feels quite messy and gross. It feels like she has hooks in you that are manipulative, toxic, draining, and unconscious. And a part of you likes that. This part likes someone being attached or hooked into you, because even if it's completely toxic, draining and dysfunctional, it makes you feel significant and attractive. It gives an insecure, needy part of you a sense of worth. It's really quite disturbing, actually, this twisted dance between you two's needy, insatiable egos."

I asked for further clarification on what this type of 'unhooking' or energetic disconnection would look like, practically.

"You need to affirm your separateness from her," Kevin explained. "First, by allowing yourself to feel all the hooks and cords still connecting the two of you, and then severing them or pulling them out of yourself. Feel all of the energy that is not yours, which you've taken on through this connection, that's still in you, without the distortion of sentimentality. Feel the toxicity of your entanglement, then push all of it out of your system. All of the foreign energy and emotion you've taken on, call it out and affirm that it isn't part of you. Use your breath, use visualization, scream profanities at the top of your lungs, do whatever feels natural to move that energy. Affirm that it's no longer welcome in you, that it no longer serves you, that it's not actually you. Fully sever your attachment and give her energy back to her. You're doing this all to restore your sense of self and your boundaries. And it might take a while, just keep on pulling out hooks, cutting cords, giving the feelings a voice and pushing out energy that isn't yours until it's done."

"And how will I know when I'm done?" I asked.

"You'll be back in your light. You'll be grounded in yourself. You'll just feel it."

I wasn't sure I understood what that meant, but Kevin assured me I'd know it when it happened, offering no further explanation. Kevin was so firmly rooted in the reality of energy that this was all just a normal, everyday thing to him. For me it was completely new, and required that I suspend my disbelief and fumble around in the unknown. Since I was going to have some time on my hands over the coming days of solitude at my cabin (having accepted Kevin's advice to isolate myself there), it couldn't hurt to play around with and explore what he was suggesting, so I agreed to give it a shot.

That night as I lay in bed, I let go of my inhibitions and ran with everything Kevin had shared. I let myself feel the toxic, messy energy and attachments that were still active between my ex and I (there was so much raw emotion present that this didn't take much digging). I went to town visualizing myself pulling emotional hooks my ex had in me out of my body, cutting cords that were keeping us connected with cathartic slices, as well as simply feeling and pushing out the strange, heavy, dysfunctional emotional baggage that had accumulated within me. I felt myself get a little lighter with every cord I cut, and as I continued to explore and excavate the heavy, emotional gunk that had accumulated through this relationship, tears gently streamed down my cheeks. I had no idea if what I was doing was real or right, but after a while it began to feel absolutely amazing. I let myself deeply experience uncomfortable feelings I had ignored during this relationship. There were feelings and ways of being that weren't natural to me that I'd tried to blend in with, adapt to, or force myself to accept throughout this connection. I let myself feel these uncomfortable things, and then affirmed what wasn't mine and what wasn't natural to me. Following Kevin's suggestions, I attempted to create a sense of separation between my ex's energy and my own.

I don't know how long this went on for, but at some point it felt like I was finished. My face and the pillow my head was resting on were soaked with tears, and there was a deep sense that I had gotten a part of myself back. The aching sense of neediness and intertwinement with my ex that I'd been stuck in felt like it had been cleansed and soothed with tears.

After my prescribed days in isolation had passed, I decided to visit Kevin and share the progress I'd made. On my way to his house I stopped at a small park along the ocean, taking a moment to sit and enjoy the seaside view on a sunny afternoon. I'd been having some subtle feelings of anguish, regret and neediness around my ex return, so I decided to try and do a bit more of the processing Kevin had described as I sat on a park bench. Again, I let myself feel into any energy that wasn't mine and recognize it as such, and visualized myself cutting cords running between my ex and I. With my eyes closed, I saw and felt parts of my ex's pain and suffering that I didn't want to let go of, that I wanted to take care of or heal for her, and I reluctantly released my grip on them. Tears began to stream down my face, and although I once again had no idea what I was doing and if it was real or correct, when I opened my wet eyes there was a feeling of gentleness, calm and purity in me that was quite notable.

As I sat on a park bench and collected myself, Kevin appeared on his bike, carrying a bag of brownies and some other sugary snacks (his diet at the time seemed to be largely composed of desserts). He immediately asked me what had just happened, commenting that my energy looked "shockingly good". When I told him about what I'd just done, and my experience back at the cabin a couple of nights earlier, he said: "Oh, you've just cleared your energy. You should be doing that several times a day, minimum."

Chapter Two

I still really didn't know what I'd done or what he was talking about, but nodded in agreement. That sounded about right.

With the update on my emotional process out of the way, Kevin was eager to talk about what was next for me. In particular, he wanted to talk about the five women he'd felt waiting in the ether months earlier when we first discussed my love life. They were still there, he said, and he could feel one of them in particular quite strongly.

"Wow, I'm pretty sure you have already met her, or she is going to be showing up in your world within the next week." He paused to eat a brownie and closed his eyes as though to look closer as something. "Thursday! Expect her to arrive in your world on Thursday! Yep, it's very clear."

With my breakup so fresh and raw, I wasn't sure I wanted a new lover to show up on Thursday, though. That felt way too soon. I tried to explain this to Kevin, telling him that I didn't feel ready or able to meet someone new.

"Your energy doesn't say that," he responded. "You are completely ready. You've been ready since we first talked about this months ago, and the emotional work you just did has gotten you even more prepared. You can say whatever you want from your brain, but your energy is speaking loud and clear on this, Miles. Not only are you ready, but she is already on the way. Can't you feel what I'm saying? Seriously, take a moment and feel into it. I'm talking about something very real. You should be able to sense it just as clearly as me."

Feeling somewhat trapped and under pressure from Kevin, I began to silently probe myself while he patiently waited, not really knowing what I was looking for. Part of me was filled with curiosity and hope around what we were talking about, while another part was closed and totally uninterested. Nothing in me felt clear as I sat and focused inward.

"Let me ask you this again, more directly," Kevin interjected. "Can you feel what I'm feeling? Can you feel the energy I'm talking about? It's palpable, it's real, and you should be able to feel it clearly. Just let yourself be completely honest and tell me what you feel."

Kevin had an intensity in this moment which was both encouraging and intimidating. As I closed my eyes and tried to look within, I teetered back and forth between freezing under pressure, and cluelessly fumbling around in the dark of my awareness.

"Can you feel her?" Kevin asked once again. I told him I had no idea, and he started to get impatient.

"Miles, imagine I have a loaded gun to your head. I'm holding it against your temple, and if you lie, I pull the trigger. Nothing but complete honesty is allowed here. And that includes not saying 'I don't know' when you do know. Do you understand?" I nodded. "You lie, you die," he continued. "Now let me ask you again: Do you know who this person is already? Can you feel them?"

A few minutes earlier, when I had initially began to look inward, a woman had instantly come to my mind. I didn't think this meant anything other than that I was interested in her, though, and brushed it off as meaningless. With Kevin's intensity and insistence bearing down on me, I reluctantly shared that there was one person who had come to mind, and that I had met her briefly once before. Her name was Robynne, and we'd been introduced to one another a few months earlier at a gathering of mutual friends. I remembered her clearly because when I looked into Robynne's eyes at that gathering, it felt as though I was looking into a fire that was burning into the very core of my being. The sensation was so powerful that I actually found it hard to look at her - I could only bear the intensity of it for seconds before I had to avert my eyes. I was in a relationship at the time, so didn't try to get to know her deeply. In fact I tried to not get too familiar with her, because the feeling I had experienced when our eyes met was so intense and did not seem platonic by any stretch of the imagination.

Once I shared this with Kevin, his interrogation continued.

"Okay, excellent. So is this her? Is this the next love in your life? Is Robynne the person who's coming on Thursday? Remember, if you lie you die. There's a gun to your head. Just feel the energy and be honest."

I had no idea how to answer this question. How could I know? Kevin, however, kept pushing.

"Miles, you don't have to guess here. Just go into the energy - feel her energy. You know what her energy feels like quite clearly, because you two connected in such a strong way. Connect to her energy and ask if she wants to be in your life. Ask if she would like to be your new romantic partner, and if she is going to show up in your world to make that happen."

With Kevin pushing me so forcefully, my inhibitions started to blur somewhat, and I let him walk me into having a conversation with the energy of a woman who I didn't know at all. I closed my eyes and tried to focus on what Robynne felt like - on her energy. It was actually easier than I thought, since she'd made such a strong impression on me.

"Good, you can feel her energy," Kevin said. "Now ask if she wants to be your partner, and let me know what she says. No filtering, just say what you feel from her."

I threw caution to the wind and asked. It's difficult to explain what exactly I was interacting with at this point, but the best way to describe it is that I had focused on the burning energy I felt while in Robynne's presence, and it was as though I was talking to it. And when I asked it the simple question Kevin suggested, the answer was an instant, unambiguous yes. More questions followed from Kevin, and more answers came as I sat with my eyes closed and tears beginning to stream down my face. The main information I got through this was that Robynne was indeed the person who would be my next girlfriend, she was going to show up in my world soon, and she was really excited about this. The whole experience was bizarre, surreal, and disorienting. Afterwards, I didn't know what to make of it. It was certainly an interesting exploration, but putting any stock in what I had felt when reaching out into the ethers (or my imagination) seemed like a stretch to me. Kevin, on the other hand, needed no convincing.

"Everything you said checked out energetically one hundred percent. Couldn't you feel that? Robynne's going to be showing up on Thursday, and she's your next girlfriend, that's obvious."

To him none of this was a guess or an intuitive hunch, it was an observable reality that just hadn't come into form yet.

The following Thursday, I received an invitation from Robynne (who was basically a stranger that I was not in any regular contact with at the time) to a housewarming party at her new home. Kevin was completely unsurprised, and considered it a confirmation of what he and I had both felt during our process in the park. I tried to discount it as a coincidence, saying that it was just an invite to an event, and it didn't mean she was actually seriously interested in me.

Kevin's only response to this was to say: "Miles, you're being an idiot."

As things unfolded over the following weeks and months, Robynne and I did meet and quickly formed an incredibly close, loving relationship. Without going into great detail, almost as quickly as we got into this close relationship, we also discovered differences that eventually made us decide to just be friends. That experience is in itself a whole other story that I won't share here, but in the arc of my journey with Kevin, the exactitude with which he foresaw it was another head-scratching demonstration of his gifts. I couldn't wrap my mind around how he was so tuned into the energy of everything, and why this was all happening in my life.

Chapter Three

As I began to spend more time around Kevin, I quickly lost interest in my life in the woods. Where I previously had endless enthusiasm to tend my little vegetable garden or learn a variety of archaic bushcraft skills, suddenly most of my attention was being drawn in a new direction. Kevin was so magnetic, unusual, and interesting that my trips to his and Daniel's home grew in frequency until I was visiting them nearly every day.

Life in his world was always steeped with meaning, and there was always some new revelation being uncovered. Nothing was mundane, every day I would witness some astonishing feat of intuition or unbelievable synchronicity that defied explanation and stretched my mind open.

But as much as I was drawn to Kevin, I also questioned almost everything that came out of his mouth, and disagreed with much of it. Our world views were completely different, and we were both relatively strong-willed, opinionated individuals. As a result, much of the first summer I knew Kevin was spent in extensive daily debates that took place on the grass of his front yard. These conversations often stretched on for hours, and were the meeting of two disparate and totally incompatible world views.

On my end was the belief that the modern world was basically a terrible mess, a calamity of injustice and tragedy that had no rhyme or reason. I viewed the natural world as a sanctuary of grace and beauty, and saw humanity as at best hopelessly lost, and at worst evil and depraved, woefully at odds with nature and everything sacred. This wasn't a terribly optimistic vision of human life on earth, but I was deeply committed to it. My motivation to live in the woods, removed from the clamour and confusion of modern society, was rooted in this misanthropic perspective.

Kevin, on the other hand, saw everything about every aspect of life on earth as part of a perfect divine order. He believed that every experience, whether tragic or ecstatic, was carefully constructed for the evolution of the soul experiencing it. To him, life on Earth was a stage for the evolution of souls, and all the dramas of the human experience were simply divine orchestrations that facilitated this learning and growth. Tragedy could serve this, as could reconciliation, joy, and peace. Literally every experience could (and does) serve this.

One might define my worldview as deeply earthbound and misanthropic, in the sense that what mattered most to me was the material or natural world (it was basically my god) and I saw humanity as more or less a scourge on it, an aberration from the sacred natural order.

Kevin's worldview was the opposite. He saw the earth as merely a playground for souls to evolve on, that functioned more like an energetic hologram than the dense physical world I believed in. He still believed in the beauty and sanctity of all life on earth and nature itself, but saw our reality as simply energy, changing from moment to moment, adapting to the energy and emotion of the perceiver. Nothing in this reality was a mistake or tragedy, it was all part of some brilliant bigger picture.

Chapter Three

Where I saw the current state of life on earth as a senseless mess, and looked at history as a series of falls further and further from grace, Kevin saw perfection. He saw consciousness evolving through new and profound scenarios. He saw souls learning through conflict, hearts expanding in their capacity to love through the excruciating experience of its absence and opposite. He saw purpose in all tragedy and suffering, he saw purpose in every experience. And he saw every human, even in their most depraved moment, as a soul on an exquisite learning journey.

Nearly every day that summer we would sit down to debate from these two viewpoints, and I was convinced every time we did so that I was about to clobber Kevin. There was honestly never any doubt in my mind whatsoever that Kevin was about to be humbled, perhaps due to the fact that I was usually able to easily persuade others when I believed something strongly. This never once turned out to be the case during these conversations, however.

I don't know if I would have admitted it at the time, but Kevin generally ran laps around me during these exchanges, as I scratched my head and fumbled for thoughts. I had a few emotionally charged big ideas that I could huff and puff around, but when they were deeply examined and questioned, there was actually very little substance behind them.

Kevin's worldview, however, was much more integrated and coherent. He had an instant, effortless response to each and every challenge I presented to him. In retrospect, I'm not sure he ever actually considered any of these conversations debates. He might have just thought he was teaching me, because he was at such an unfair advantage once we actually got into the details of any subject. And while I was arrogant enough to assume myself smarter than Kevin, when he casually poked holes in my arguments, I was humble enough to admit it.

37

One day I brought up a series of tragedies as examples of senseless misery, proof that there was not a divine order to the madness of the world. The first example I referenced was an ongoing, massive, offshore oil spill happening in the Gulf of Mexico at the time. I asked Kevin how one could possibly see anything good coming out of such a senseless disaster?

"It's going to raise people's consciousness," he replied. "There are going to be changes that come out of it. Businesses and people are going to have to face some hard truths. It's going to change the people who live in that area. An enormous amount of good can come out of it. It might take more disasters, and worse disasters. This one alone may only move mass consciousness a tiny nudge towards bigger change and more integrity, but mass consciousness is evolving through it."

This was essentially Kevin's reply to the majority of my challenges, and I never had a good rebuttal. As this particular debate continued, I reached for other historical examples of irredeemable atrocity to prove life was unfair and senseless. It almost didn't matter what example of genocide, injustice, greed or corruption I brought up, Kevin's response was generally a slight variation on the same theme: "It's consciousness evolving," he would say. "All of that pain, all of the trauma that was endured and introduced and continues to circulate, it's all providing the opportunity for souls to grow in extraordinary ways. And yes, trauma, pain, and absolutely disgusting things that should never happen to anyone, anywhere, happen to people as part of this. It is heartbreaking. I am not excusing or minimizing anyone being hurt or violated. But it doesn't happen in vain. Consciousness evolves through it, and you have to understand what an extraordinary thing that really is."

I didn't like this argument or agree with it, but I had nothing solid to counter it with, and would end up walking away from most of our conversations with my tail between my legs as a result.

At the end of one of these conversations, Kevin asked me a question: "Whether you agree with me or not Miles, tragedy happens. Trauma happens. It's part of life here. Whose response to it leads to a better place? Yours: Where because of this we lose all trust in life and humanity, close our hearts to the world, and become married to anger, resentment, and hatred? Or, the alternative that I'm holding: Where we look for the lesson in our pain, where we decide that there's a sacred purpose in our suffering, and that we can grow into wiser, stronger, more beautiful people through fully facing and moving through it? Where we grow into a deeper connection to love through adversity, instead of closing our hearts in response to it? In the perspective I'm holding, we still get to have boundaries, we still get to stand up to injustice and live with integrity, but there's a bigger picture within which everything fits. There is a meaning and grace to *everything*. Which one of these responses to life do you think leads to better results for an individual, and the world?"

I chose to pass on this question, though his point was duly noted.

Where my position really unraveled was when we shifted away from looking at bigger picture, abstract situations, and brought our focus back onto the reality of my own personal experience.

"Your life is an ongoing demonstration of everything I'm talking about, Miles," Kevin would say. "Everything happening in your world - the car accident, the book deal, ending your relationship and then Robynne showing up in its wake - all of this was completely organized to match where your energy was at, the choices you were making, and the lessons you were learning."

For years I'd thought of this type of spiritual philosophy as delusional and childish. Given everything that had been happening in my world, however, I found myself unable to argue with Kevin on the matter, and unsure of what I even believed anymore.

The other weakness in my side of the debate, where things fully came undone, was the matter of my unexamined wounds and projections. Whenever Kevin spoke to these, he had me in checkmate. A common example during one of our heated conversations would look like this: "Miles, let's just step back for a second, because your energy is getting crazy as you talk about your perspective on the world. Here's the thing: You grew up in an environment that felt unfair. Your experience with authority was that it can't be trusted. It betrayed you. Your formative experiences with people taught you that they are cruel, judgemental and closed-hearted. Now, as an adult, having left that early environment, you see the whole world this way. You've never stopped to own or process those formative experiences, so they continue to colour everything you see. It's just simple projection. I'm not saying anything profound, but at the same time, the implications of it for you are absolutely profound. I mean, you went and lived alone in the woods for years because of this, because of your unprocessed pain. You've closed your heart to the world and much of humanity because of it. And let's be clear, almost nothing you have believed about life, about humanity or the true nature of this world is correct. It's based on the little fragment of experience that caused your wounds. And when you finally are able to see, own and heal those wounds, you'll understand that even they are a part of something loving and divine. *Everything is*, no exceptions. But because you haven't even begun to examine these parts of yourself, you're still believing an illusion formed from pain, shame, trauma and fear. You don't actually see the world, you see yourself."

Chapter Three

Checkmate.

Generally speaking, every argument and counter-argument I made would be poked through. There was always a hole, some bigger picture I wasn't seeing, some opportunity at a heart or soul level I'd neglected to appreciate. The main problem was that I hadn't looked at the human experience from a bigger perspective. Another way of saying this is that I hadn't given much thought to what life is really about, at the deepest level. Kevin contended that it was about the heart being opened and evolving a greater capacity for love, grace, authenticity and compassion. It made sense that a person who has walked through the valleys of suffering, despair and grief, then emerged on the other side, may have a heart that is wider and wiser than the person who hasn't travelled through such wastelands of the soul.

"We're all just souls learning and growing here, Miles. That's all this is. And everything here is perfectly and divinely arranged to meet the soul where it's at on this journey, moment to moment. Physical reality simply arranges itself to fulfil this dance. Everything is divinely ordered in this reality, mark my words."

This was Kevin's paradigm in a nutshell, and one thing that touched me was that it wasn't a philosophy to him. It wasn't an idea or a spiritual concept - Kevin felt the energy of an individual, and could see how that energy would ripple out and shape their reality. It's how he knew my book would be published right away, and how he knew I would get hurt (and eventually be killed) when I was dating someone wildly wrong for me.

One day, after a long debate session, Kevin said: "Miles, the difference between you and me is that you're a philosopher, and I'm a prophet. You *think*, I *know*. None of this is speculative for me. This is reality." He then stood up in front of me, with his feet planted on the ground just over shoulder-width apart, knees slightly bent, and pointed at his groin with both hands, staring menacingly into my eyes and raising his voice: "If you can prove me wrong, I will stand before you, and you can kick me in the balls as hard as possible!" That was Kevin's way of showing his conviction. And in case you were wondering, I never did get the opportunity to prove him wrong and execute that kick.

While there were certain concepts Kevin held that I couldn't wrap my head around, the underlying notion that everything in my own life was designed for my soul to grow through was something I gradually warmed to. I could appreciate looking at the devastations of my love life, my sordid childhood experience or the society I'd rejected and ran away from all as parts of something brilliantly designed to facilitate my heart's expansion.

One significant detail about Kevin that makes this all the more interesting, is that he was chronically sick. For the entire time that I knew him, he suffered from chronic Lyme disease. One way this manifested was extreme sensitivities to any scent or fragrance. Traces of shampoo, perfume or laundry soap would give him intense migraines, sometimes putting him in bed for days at a time. He also suffered from a severe electromagnetic sensitivity. This caused him to experience neurological pain, migraines and brain fog as a result of such ordinary things as looking at a computer screen for any amount of time, being under fluorescent lights or riding in a car. Because of these and other symptoms and sensitivities, a day never went by when Kevin wasn't in extreme physical pain. He was always exploring ways of healing himself, and probing into deeper emotional issues that he suspected could be related to why he was sick in the first place.

It amazed me that despite his own profound and debilitating chronic suffering, he remained the most vociferous defender of life's ultimate fairness, divine purpose and perfection I had ever met. His conviction was completely unshakeable, even under the weight of his enduring pain.

By the end of that first summer with Kevin, my life was beginning to change. I was no longer fixated on the forest and a life on the land as an ideal. I wasn't sure what my ideal was anymore, all I knew is that there was something else showing up, and it might actually contain the things I'd gone to nature trying to find in the first place.

This was a very exciting, joyful and inspiring time in my life. What was about to come, however, was quite a bit more challenging and humbling than anything I had imagined. In retrospect, all of the interesting and magical things that initially happened with Kevin might have simply helped prime me for all of the difficult and humiliating stuff to follow.

Chapter Four

One afternoon while walking to Kevin and Daniel's house, I passed by the local health food store and saw a car pulling out of the parking lot with several paper bags full of groceries sitting precariously on its roof. I recognized the man driving as a local busker who often played his acoustic guitar on busy sidewalks around town. He was usually accompanied by his baby daughter while busking, who slept in a stroller beside him as he played folk songs for passersby.

As he drove out of the parking lot, I realized that this man had been distracted (maybe by his daughter), and his entire load of groceries, wobbling on the edge of his car's roof, was going to be strewn on the road behind him in the very near future.

Shouting and waving my arms in the air as he drove away, I began to sprint as fast as I could to try and catch up with him. When he stopped at an intersection, I was able to arrive alongside him, knock on his window, and let him know the precarious position his groceries were in. He was sincerely thankful, we exchanged a laugh, shook hands, and that was that.

When I got to Kevin and Daniel's house a short while later, I described to them what had just happened, mostly because I felt proud of doing a good deed. I then casually mentioned that I was surprised by the fact that I actually felt compelled to help this guy out in the first place.

They were both confused by this comment, and asked me to explain. I told them that normally, I would have just let the chips fall as they may and wouldn't have felt any urge to step in and help a stranger in such a scenario. I didn't really care if a stranger suffered some minor hardship. I was basically a misanthrope, bitter and cynical about humanity in general. I felt people were overall pretty awful, so why help? I wasn't a full-blown sociopath, and certainly some individuals could stir my empathy more than others (children, the elderly and the marginalized), but it wouldn't have been unusual for me to feel like I couldn't care less about some random guy's groceries.

Kevin and Daniel were both shocked by this, yet to my mind it was totally rational. I was more surprised at my spontaneous act of kindness, and had to admit that it felt good. Kevin seemed to think the fact that this was unusual or out of character for me spoke volumes. He and Daniel agreed that rushing to help this man was just a normal thing to do, unquestionable really. They couldn't imagine not having helped were they in a similar position.

"It's just highlighting the part of you that is underdeveloped," Kevin said.

Curious to know exactly what he was getting at with this comment, I asked him to explain what part of me he was referring to.

"You have an underdeveloped heart, Miles. It's closed off, cold, and keeps you from feeling connected to others. You seem to open it up to lovers in a fairly deep way, but excluding a few specific, narrow circumstances, the rest of the time it's often ice-cold and cemented shut. It can be brutal and harsh in its coldness."

Daniel was simply a silent bystander at this point, but was clearly in agreement with every word Kevin said.

"Think of the Grinch who stole Christmas, and how his heart was a few sizes on the small size. That's exactly what I'm talking about here, that's the perfect analogy for you."

Kevin continued explaining my heart's apparent lack of development from several angles, and as I sat and listened I felt a mixture of confusion, incredulity, shame and annoyance. My self-perception was that of a somewhat enlightened person. I'd spent a significant amount of time living alone in the woods, and had many profound, revelatory experiences during these periods. Generally, because of my unusual life path, I considered myself more wise and self-aware than basically everyone around me. And yet here I was listening to this guy tell me I was a living embodiment of the Grinch who stole Christmas? None of it lined up.

Even more frustrating to me was the fact that Kevin didn't have any of the experiences or attributes that I felt a more enlightened person should. He had never lived close to nature. He didn't eat a conscious, healthy diet (he lived primarily off Chinese takeout, Coca-Cola, desserts, potato chips and chocolate bars at the time). He wasn't celibate (on the contrary, he spoke openly and without shame about watching porn and other seemingly unenlightened carnal pleasures). His lifestyle seemed to fly in the face of many of the superficial rules and expectations I had for an awakened individual, whereas mine more or less lined up with many of them.

"I can see you aren't liking what I'm saying and it isn't getting in," Kevin continued. "But Miles, trust me, you want to hear these words. You will be thanking me one day for telling you this, as much as a part of you is hating me for it right now. Your heart wants attention, it wants to develop. This isn't bad news, it's great news, because there's an opportunity for you to change if you can actually see where you're at."

I left this interaction certain, once again, that there were some things Kevin just didn't see right.

Around this time, Daniel came across a book that he got quite excited about, and everyone in our circle of friends, including Kevin, took turns reading it and talking about the general concept it presented. It was written by a psychic named Ainslie MacLeod, whose work involved spirit guides and past lives, two spiritual concepts that Kevin had no strong interest in and rarely ever spoke about.

The central premise of this book provided some fuel for interesting and fun conversations. The main idea was that everyone has a soul age, and this soul age is something that exists independent from their biological age or experience in this lifetime. It is a more transcendental, essential maturity that each individual brings with them into this life at a soul level. This soul maturity is accumulated over many lifetimes, as a soul goes through a variety of incarnations. The older a soul gets (by experiencing a diverse range of lives), generally the more gracious, compassionate, wise, and unfazed by the disorienting influences of their environment they become. The older souls are more firmly connected to their truth, their heart, and their authentic nature, while the younger souls are more brittle, more insecure and egoic. Younger souls are more competitive, less connected to their personal truth, less capable of seeing and honouring the sanctity of others, and much more easily tempted and intoxicated by the lure of power, money, social acceptance, sex, fame and whatnot.

The book laid out a simple soul age grading system of sorts, where a level-one soul was the youngest and least developed type of soul, and a level-ten was the oldest. It was a somewhat crude and reductive scale, but the author argued that making a soul age scale that was truly comprehensive in its breadth and depth would be mind-bogglingly complex. Therefore, a simplistic ten-level system was preferred.

I wasn't sure if I believed in past lives, but still found great fun and enjoyment in playing around with these concepts, particularly when it came to exploring what each of our personal soul ages were. Kevin, being the hyper-empath, already had his own clear impressions of everyone's soul age, which made this exercise all the more interesting.

On a scale of one to ten, Daniel seemed to unanimously be considered a level-ten soul by everyone. At first I was a little dubious of this, because he didn't have any of the superficial traits I attributed to a more enlightened type of person. He was lazy, socially awkward, hedonistic and generally directionless.

Kevin, however, was unequivocal in his assessment. "It's because his heart is so pure that he hasn't been able to put himself together in this life yet," he said. "Daniel was so devastated early on in life, his whole sense of self was shattered to pieces, and it's precisely because his heart is so profound and beautiful that he got so confused and disoriented. And yet within that disorientation, he is still an incredibly gentle, pure, loving man. Within his dysfunction he is still tender, deeply empathetic and graceful. It's absolutely incredible."

So Daniel got top honours on the soul age scale. Kevin was also considered a level-ten soul, but no one was surprised by that. His capacity for empathy and understanding were remarkable, and his intuitive prowess seemed to be exactly what one would expect from a senior soul.

My younger brother Lonnie even got brought into this discussion, and the consensus was that he was another level-ten soul. A couple of other close friends were part of the process, and the results were the same - all tens, though everyone had a different personal flair or flavour.

Then it came to me. I'm not sure why, but Kevin and I were alone in his living room when the subject of my soul age was broached. It seemed that he had given a strong opinion on everyone's soul age but mine, so I asked for his thoughts on where I stood on this matter. He replied that he had a very clear sense of my soul age, but wanted me to go inward and find what felt true for myself before he shared his thoughts.

That sounded like a good idea, so I relaxed my mind, closed my eyes, and focused on the question at hand. Almost immediately the number seven registered in my awareness. It wasn't what I had expected, but after waiting in silence for a while, I decided to share it anyway. When I told Kevin that seven was the only thing coming to me, he shared that he had felt the same thing, saying that I was "about a seven."

Then, suddenly, it dawned on me: I was a seven, and everyone else was a ten. *That's not good!* I was supposed to be wiser and more enlightened than everyone, this couldn't be right.

Kevin assured me, however, that it was right. "You have a less developed heart, Miles. Just think of the other day when you were surprised by your willingness to help out that stranger with his groceries. That's how you know your heart has some growing to do. Your capacity to shut people out, the way you can be ruled by your pain, frustration and anger, it's all younger soul stuff."

The matter of me being a mere level-seven soul quickly became a running joke amongst everyone. The worst part of this was that it was me who had actually called myself a seven. I'd seen it and named it all on my own.

While none of us took this rather crude, reductive measuring system very seriously, it was still a hit to my ego, my sense of superiority and sophistication. I was being challenged to see myself as less developed than everyone around me in a fundamental way, and I was not loving it.

According to the book we'd been passing around, one's soul level changes through successive life experiences accumulated across centuries and millennia, through the trials and tribulations of various lifetimes or incarnations. So my lowly soul level of seven seemed to be an immutable deficit, at least for this incarnation. It was something I couldn't change in a meaningful way this time around. It would take many incarnations, spanning many centuries, for it to change.

Kevin, however, strongly disagreed with this assessment, suggesting that such a slow timeline of change accounted for a lot of "laziness and unconsciousness."

"You absolutely can evolve very far beyond where you are now in this lifetime, there is no limit whatsoever on how far you can go. It will just require unusual choices, but it seems like you're already okay with those. Everyone is growing no matter what they choose to do in this life, but most people grow at an incredibly slow pace. They stay in the same unquestioned and unexamined lessons for a whole lifetime in some instances. A good example of this would be a marriage or job that continues for decades after its expiry date - a situation where a person languishes in something familiar and comfortable, but totally malnourishing to their soul, rather than challenging themselves to move forward and grow. The kind of change you are asking about is completely different from that. It requires aggressively embracing your truth and turning towards your feelings, turning towards your heart and whatever blocks it, and living from a place of courage and honesty. To me, nothing else is actually acceptable. It's not easy, and parts of you will fight it as though their existence depends on remaining stuck. And those parts aren't entirely wrong, they do have to burn and change. But of course you get to grow massively in this life if you choose to Miles, why else do you think you are here? Why do you think we're talking about this? Why do you think I showed up in your life?"

In my conversations with Daniel on this subject, he couldn't wrap his head around why I thought being a level-seven soul was such a bad thing.

"That's like being thirty years old and wishing you were sixty," he said. "It doesn't make any sense to me. Every age is awesome, and a younger age has some amazing things that older age doesn't. There's no better or worse."

That was a rather sobering perspective. Typical of a level-ten soul, I thought.

Although none of us took this simple soul-level concept completely seriously, it was facilitating a glimpse into a bigger picture of who I was, and acted as a small blow to my armour. In retrospect, it was just foreshadowing all that was about to come.

Kevin and I were having a conversation on his front lawn one evening when a group of young women walked past us and caught my attention. For a moment, our conversation paused. I recognized one of the women as someone I'd seen before and shared some mutual friends with, otherwise they were just three attractive women walking by. I smiled and made eye contact with the one woman I recognized, and after the momentary distraction, my attention returned to Kevin, whose mood had dramatically changed during the brief pause in our conversation.

"I just saw a part of you I really don't like, Miles," Kevin shared with a sense of disdain.

I was sincerely confused by this. Nothing had happened that I was aware of in the previous moments to make him say such a thing.

"You aren't aware of what your energy just did?" Kevin asked.

I wasn't aware of anything. Nothing happened so far as I was concerned.

Kevin proceeded to explain that he'd just watched me turn into a kind of monster, energetically. When those young women passed, he claimed my heart had completely shut down to him and cut him out, so to speak. In an instant, he felt me transform from a friend to a rival, as a very primal, instinctive program in me was initiated, where all that mattered was that I receive attention and energy from those passing women.

"Imagine the most stereotypical, meathead alpha male, walking down the street with his shirt off, massive swollen muscles on display to attract attention and stoke his ego. That's who you just became. Competitive, mean, vain and closed-hearted. Suddenly I was as good as dead to you. I was mere competition for the attention and energy you craved. All empathy for me completely vanished. Can't you feel that?"

I had absolutely no idea what Kevin was talking about. Was this just his insecurity talking? The women had seemingly been looking and smiling at me, not him, after all. On one hand, the idea that this was simply Kevin's own discomfort with himself was an easy story to believe. He remained adamant about what he saw, though. To him, this was a teachable moment.

"Feel your energy Miles - can't you feel that you're still triggered? Can't you feel how your heart is closed to me?"

It was as though he was asking a blind person to describe the landscape before them - I wanted to say no, you're wrong, or yes, you're right, but I had no idea what he was talking about.

He continued: "What do you feel in your body right now? What's going on physiologically?"

I took a moment to think about this before responding: "I feel like I'm being put on the spot. I think I just feel annoyed that you make a big deal out of everything."

Kevin shook his head, "You're too far gone for now. You're totally in your wound. This is exactly what you need to see though, so let me be very clear about this: The part of you I just saw is disturbing. He lacks integrity, he is unsophisticated, his heart is cold and calculating, all he cares about are his shallow, vain desires, and he will stomp on the vulnerability and purity of others with no conscience in pursuit of them."

When Kevin had finished naming the part of me he was so disturbed by, his mood once again suddenly shifted. Returning to an upbeat and friendly tone, he remarked how wonderful it felt to get that all off his chest. "It's so important to share the truth," he said, and we proceeded to part ways for the evening.

This conversation seemed to mark the beginning of a new chapter in my connection with Kevin. Perhaps he'd just seen something in me more clearly than before, or he felt that I was now ready to hear about it more directly, but from that afternoon on, Kevin seemed to become much more aggressive in his critique of my character. Where before spending time around him had been a generally uplifting and inspiring experience, it now transitioned to being more humbling, often painfully so.

I wasn't sure I liked this change, or whether I agreed with what he was saying, and so for a while my visits became less frequent.

One thing that made it particularly challenging for me to accept Kevin's more critical insights into my character was the reality of his own imperfections. Kevin's life was an ongoing struggle, as he navigated a variety of inner conflicts and personal issues.

Chapter Four

At times it was hard to see the complexity and wounds of the messenger, and remain open to receiving their message (especially when that message stung).

On many occasions, I witnessed friends and acquaintances shake their heads and walk away from Kevin when they saw how fraught with difficulty his life was, while he offered a penetrating critique of theirs. I was often tempted to do the same, but whenever that temptation arose, my curiosity was far too strong for me to walk away. The light that Kevin held was so fascinating, and represented such an adventure, challenge, and mystery to me, that I couldn't resist seeing where it might lead, even with his struggles and imperfections in plain sight. And as much as part of me didn't like how it felt to receive a certain kind of feedback from him, I couldn't seem to help myself from going back for more.

During this time, the book of mine that Kevin had made bold predictions about was published. Within the small subculture that it was geared towards, it was showing promising signs of being modestly successful. One twist to this was that my interest in and affinity with the material I'd written in the book had more or less vanished by the time it was published. There were elements of it that I was still close to, but by and large I'd outgrown the perspective from which I had created it, and I was growing further away from it each day. Eventually, this would mean stepping away from my life and work related to that book, leaving it to languish and fade away. Despite all of this, the experience of putting writing out into the world and having others respond positively to it was significant.

One day I was talking with Kevin and mentioned a book-related speaking engagement I was going to be flying out of the country to do, when his mood once again shifted.

"Miles, you're letting this all go to your head," he stated. "The faint whiff of success you're experiencing is feeding the brutish alpha male part of you, inflating your ego, and it's frankly disturbing to watch."

Once again, I had no idea what Kevin was talking about. There was nothing I was aware of doing or feeling that would suggest anything he described was at play in me.

"It's in your energy, Miles," he continued. "There is a smugness, an arrogance, and it's quite strong and toxic. The problem is that you aren't outwardly doing anything you would consider toxic with it, so you can fool yourself into believing it's not there or it doesn't matter. But believe me, it's at the driver's seat of your consciousness. It's totally in control. It's been present in our entire interaction today. Your inflated ego is functioning like a barrier that keeps you from being connected with and grounded to the sanctity of everyone around you. And that fact alone means it is real and causing harm in your world."

I was getting to the point where Kevin's admonitions about my ego and closed heart were becoming annoying, and decided to push back, suggesting that Kevin was jealous or insecure about my tiny modicum of success, and that nothing he was saying made any sense. I became quite heated, and said that what he claimed to be seeing simply didn't ring true - I wasn't being overtaken by greed or vanity. I wasn't suffering from an over-inflated ego. He was flat wrong.

Kevin responded by asking: "Miles, do you realize you're triggered right now?" This is a question I would go on to receive from him countless times (the meaning of being triggered, in this context, is that an unresolved emotional wound, unrelated to the reality of the present moment, has been activated and is altering one's perception of the present moment).

My blood was burning with frustration and anger, my jaw was clenched, my mind flooded with emotion and geared in one direction only: Pushing back with maximum force. Given all of this, I responded in the most obvious way, aggressively snapping: "No! I'm not triggered at all!"

We went back and forth for God knows how long, Kevin patiently trying to show me how I was triggered, followed by me becoming more upset and indignant with each of his observations.

Our argument ended with Kevin making a passionate plea: "Miles, you have to believe me here, what I'm showing you is the key to heaven on earth. It is the key to you receiving everything your heart has ever wanted. You must see the arrogant part of yourself I'm shining a light on very clearly if you don't want to live a life ruled by fear, insecurity and pain. Until you learn to own these parts of yourself, they will rule you, and you'll remain a fragmented, weak person. I'm not simply trying to tear you down, I'm trying to show you a better way. I'm your friend here."

I left this conversation once again confused and annoyed. Why couldn't Kevin just be happy with my meagre accomplishments? And why did he tell me I was triggered every time I challenged his all-seeing eyes? One of us had to be wrong, and as far as I could tell, it was obviously him.

At this point, I began inquiring among friends to see if they could verify or disprove Kevin's assessment of me and my underdeveloped heart. Daniel was of little help here. He seemed to agree with Kevin, but was too afraid of how I might react to be completely straight and honest about his feelings. In retrospect, the fact that he was so frightened by my potentially volatile reaction should have probably spoken volumes to me. I asked one of my ex-girlfriends, but she was an unreliable

witness and told me as much, as we'd both projected all kinds
of angelic qualities onto each other that blinded us to what was
real, ugly or hard to look at.

The more I asked around, however, the more feedback I
received to make me suspect that Kevin might actually be
seeing something I simply wasn't. He also might be seeing
something others were too afraid to openly acknowledge, or
were too consumed by their own insecurities and egos to see
clearly. After talking to a dozen or so friends, I came away with
my tail between my legs more or less. None of them said
anything nearly as damning as Kevin had, but each described
some aspect of what he was pointing to - a capacity to close off,
be harsh, mean, competitive, scary, or otherwise act like a
person that contradicted the essence of who and what I
thought I was.

Shortly after my heated exchange with Kevin, I was visiting
him and Daniel when I asked what his thoughts on my book
were. I'd given him a copy of it almost a month earlier, and he
was quite excited and eager to read it, considering he was
instrumental in getting it into print.

He was clearly uncomfortable when I brought this subject
up, confessing that he'd avoided talking about my book
because he found it so repulsive. Never one to soften the truth,
Kevin gave a searing, devastating review of my book, or the
tiny fraction of it he'd been able to stomach looking at. He
couldn't bear to read a substantial amount of it because, in his
words, the energy was so incredibly toxic.

"I'm sorry Miles, it feels bad to say this, but the whole thing
is filled with your unprocessed anger, harshness and rage. The
energy is basically akin to reading hate literature, it's so brutal,
mean and misguided. In essence, hate literature is exactly what
it is - you have unhealed wounds and throughout the book
you project that pain towards innocent and inappropriate
targets."

Chapter Four

Once again I was confused, but Kevin proceeded to paint a fairly clear picture of what he was getting at. There was an undeniable 'angry environmentalist' vibe underlying all of the writing, and what Kevin was picking up on was my own unresolved emotional pain running amok, using the subject matter and ideology of the book as its playground and justification for toxic, misdirected rage.

"There is no justification for that kind of energy running around unhinged, Miles," he said. "It's immature, closed-hearted, judgemental, arrogant, self-righteous and mean. Honestly, it's the exact energy in you that we've been talking about for the past while. I'm really sorry, but I just couldn't stomach reading your book because of it. It's that bad."

Slowly digesting what Kevin was saying, I wondered aloud why, if this was all true, there had been so much momentum around the book being published in the first place?

"I have no idea why it all happened so smoothly," Kevin responded. "Maybe it was meant to facilitate your trust in me, so you'd be open to seeing a bigger picture of life and yourself? But the book itself is garbage. You write at about a grade ten level, and bring the emotional sophistication of a neo-Nazi." He wasn't joking, and I wasn't laughing.

"To be clear, the wounded part of you that I'm talking about, and that I was so repulsed by in your writing, he deserves to be angry. His pain is real and valid. He deserves to be seen and heard, to be taken care of, supported and shown the deepest love possible. He deserves to be shown what life really is, because it isn't at all what he thinks. He's just looking through the lens of his unresolved pain, devastation, and insecurity. The pain he feels is very real, but what he's doing with it is totally inappropriate."

I sat across from Kevin, aware that much of his assessment was brutal but true, and burned in shame. Eventually I broke the silence to ask him once again why everything had flowed so gracefully if the book was so flawed? Kevin interrupted me before I could finish my question, asking: "Do you know you're triggered right now?"

Once again, my head and arms were burning with anger and shame, my jaw was tight, and my mind was flooded by a stream of emotion that wanted nothing more than to prove everyone around me wrong. Despite my inner fireworks display, I responded defensively, saying I had no idea what he was talking about.

"Miles, right now a part of you feels under attack, the way you felt for much of your childhood. A wounded part in you has been touched, and it's completely hijacking your consciousness. The story it believes right now is that I'm a bad guy, I'm mean, I'm trying to control you, judge you or hurt you, and you need to go to war to protect yourself. The energy and emotion that you're feeling is so strong that you are becoming drunk and stoned on it. You are becoming temporarily insane. You see, I did say some things that would be hard for anyone to hear, but I respect you and care for you, and would never want to hurt you or denigrate your life's work. I'm sharing what I'm sharing to help you. I know it's hard to hear, but Miles, trust me, you will be thanking me from the bottom of your heart in the future. I'm being honest with you because there's something better that the universe wants for you, not because I don't like you. I think you made something that does have a creative spark in it, and also contains a lot of unresolved pain lashing out in immature ways. There is a lot of insecurity and unexamined hurt that gets in the way of you just being you, which is where your greatest creative work will come from. Your greatest gift is your authentic self, and I want to invite you to explore another way, a way where that honesty can shine."

Still feeling a burning throughout my body and a flood of emotion blurring my mind, I asked Kevin what I was supposed to do with all of this?

"Well, you are triggered right now. You just need to not believe anything you think until you're out of that. And all of this stuff around your book, it's all part of your growth. You get to write lots of books in this lifetime, and you get to learn from your process with every one of them. You also get to ignore everything I say about them. But I can tell you, there is something absolutely massive I'm holding for you here. I'm giving you the keys to the kingdom."

After a brief silence, Kevin's tone shifted and he offered one last thought before ending our conversation: "You grew up feeling deeply unwelcome and unloved Miles, and you decided to build an armour and close your heart to protect yourself. You learned to cover your vulnerability, to hide your shame, tenderness and hurt, and in so doing a part of you mutated into this seething, brooding guy that is able to shut out others with devastating coldness. In your writing, like I said before, this part of you feels energetically identical to a neo-Nazi, even if philosophically you're the exact opposite of such a person in your beliefs. The rage, the trembling insecurity masked by harshness, the misdirected anger - these are energetically exactly the same as a skinhead. A part of you is in so much pain, it is willing to lash out in extreme ways at those it misperceives as its enemy. At certain times the enemy has been me. At other times it has been friends, authority figures, strangers, or the whole world. This pain owns you, Miles, and though it feels like a powerful force, it is the very essence of disempowerment. It's sad and I feel sorry for you, because there is a lot of hurt there, and the little, vulnerable child in you who just wants to feel welcome and loved, that guy was so neglected and dishonoured in the past, and he deserves all the love in the world. But you'll need to completely change course for him to ever receive it."

As he finished delivering his searing review of my book, Kevin returned to his normal, casual tone, and excused himself to go pick up some Chinese food.

Daniel had been a bystander to this entire conversation, and we decided to take a walk down to the river together while we discussed what had just transpired. Daniel had a unique perspective on all of this, as I'd known him since I was barely a teenager, and he'd watched me grow up. He spent countless hours at my childhood home, observing my family dynamic from an outside perspective. As we talked, he shared how obvious it was to him that Kevin's observations were true. He had witnessed me growing up feeling like a stranger, unwelcome in my own home, lacking a basic sense of belonging and acceptance, and reflected how different that was from his own experience. His family life had its own set of imperfections, but he observed how different it was from mine on this one fundamental level: He felt an unquestionable sense of belonging, love and welcomeness in his home.

As we found a bench to sit on at the riverside, Daniel ruminated on my deep feeling of being unwelcome, of being a burden, and the resentful, angry, closed heart I had developed as a result. Daniel said: "It's like your Achilles heel. You have all of these really amazing qualities as a person, but that one wound is your Achilles."

Just as Daniel finished saying these words, a man interrupted us. He was part of a group of search and rescue workers training with a rescue boat that had pulled up on the riverside near us. He was wearing a bright orange floatation suit, and went out of his way to walk up to us and ask jokingly if we'd like to come aboard the search and rescue boat and try riding the river's rapids with the rest of his crew. He had a big smile on his face that revealed he was joking, and was quite pleased with his own sense of humour.

We appreciated his joke, laughed and wished him well, and then noticed something rather bizarre: The name painted onto the side of the rescue boat he was walking back to was *Achilles* - the last word Daniel had said before we were interrupted.

Kevin would call this a textbook synchronicity, and we were both somewhat dumbfounded by it. Taking this synchronicity fairly literally, we suspected that what we had just been talking about, my Achilles, was also my lifeboat. It was probably at this point that I finally began to admit to myself that Kevin was seeing something real in me. I did, indeed, appear to have an Achilles heel that I hadn't yet owned or understood. And, it seemed, I may have found an answer to the timeless philosophical question I had been wrestling with: I was, in fact, an asshole. Now, the question was: What do I do with that?

Chapter Five

As my enthusiasm for the backwoods life I'd been living diminished, the same thing seemed to happen to my fellow landmates. One-by-one my friends moved away from our fledgling little homestead, until I was the sole remaining inhabitant. This turned out to be an ideal situation in a lot of ways, as I would visit Kevin regularly, and then return to the solitude of an empty cabin in the woods to sit with, process, and explore all that came out of our interactions.

One day during this period, I was introduced to a young woman named Preet by a mutual friend. Preet was travelling through the area and looking for a place to stay that was rustic, quiet and woodsy, and I agreed to host her as a guest. There were a couple of small, vacant cabins on the land that she could choose from to stay in, and I liked the sounds of having some company. I also found Preet very attractive, which admittedly made me all the more open to having her stay on the land.

Preet and I spent a lot of time together over the course of several days, and had great conversational chemistry. We could talk and debate over a wide range of topics for hours, totally unaware that any time had passed. While we were spending this time together, I found myself in an ongoing state of agony due to the fact that I was so attracted to Preet, and didn't know how to handle these feelings. I didn't see her as a potential partner, as she was a bit younger than me and committed to travelling. Although it felt quite clear that we weren't a match for a serious romantic relationship, that didn't make my feelings of attraction disappear. In fact the more time we spent together, going for long walks in the woods, talking at length and visiting swimming holes, the stronger my attraction grew.

In addition to our slight difference in age and her travelling lifestyle, there also seemed to be a wall up between Preet and I that prevented my feelings of attraction from naturally flowing and being expressed. The best way to describe this wall is to say that for the entire time we were around one another, a part of me didn't know if Preet hated me or not. There was a silent, pervasive sense of coldness, distance and harshness to her presence that was quite strong and intimidating. I couldn't tell if it was her insecurity coming across as a kind of protection, or if it was actually just straight, stone-cold disdain for me. Either way, because of this dynamic, we could go on wonderful long walks and carry on engaging conversations, but the whole time a part of me would be wondering if Preet absolutely hated my guts and thought I was disgusting.

When I spoke to Kevin about all of this, his feelings were mixed: "The first thing you need to do is talk to her about everything you're going through," he said. "Tell her everything you're feeling. Your sexual attraction, and how you don't see her as a partner but still have those feelings, and your discomfort around her hard emotional edge. Get it all out on the table, and you'll be amazed at what can happen. Things can completely change with simple honesty. You might have a really beautiful time together if you share what you're feeling. The wall between you two might totally transform when you bring open, honest awareness to it."

Just as Kevin finished saying this, a local man that I knew as an acquaintance, and who was sadly suffering from severe mental health issues, walked past us on the sidewalk in the distance. We only noticed him when he began screaming violent threats at me, shouting that he hated me and wanted to kill me. As he passed, Kevin and I looked at each other in shock.

"I think you'd better be careful with this girl," Kevin said. "There must be something intense and dangerous going on here. Tread very gently."

With mixed feelings, I returned to my cabin that afternoon, excited to fully share everything I'd been going through with Preet, and still a little shook from the violent outburst that had been directed towards me.

The conversation with Preet that evening went relatively well. It was painful and awkward sharing my feelings of attraction with her, and even more of a challenge owning the discomfort and apprehension I felt in her presence, but all of it was received with openness and appreciation.

Preet explained that her emotional wall was an issue that had followed her throughout her life, and though she hadn't talked about it quite so openly and directly before, she wanted very much to explore and shift it. Just talking about this dynamic immediately had the effect of making us feel a bit closer to one another.

She was also flattered by my attraction to her, and hesitantly shared that the feeling was mutual. We both agreed that it didn't seem like we would be a match as partners, but we were curious and open to exploring our mutual attraction nonetheless, with honesty, care and respect. With that all said, we decided to spend the night together, something we would have done much earlier if either of us were more willing to navigate the wall separating us and simply talk about our feelings.

The following morning, I woke up to the booming voices of two adult men laughing outside my cabin. This was extremely unusual, as the land where I lived had no road, driveway or public trail leading directly to it, and because of this, strangers seldom wandered through.

For the sake of this story, I will give a very brief description of my living situation at the time: It would be simplest to say that my friends and I had made an unofficial agreement with the owner of the land where we lived. They knew about our presence on their land and the cabins that we'd built on it, and were supportive of our existence there. But they turned a blind eye to us in any official sense, not formally acknowledging we were there and not collecting any rent. We were essentially given permission to do as we pleased, and they would pretend we weren't there, as they felt that we were a beneficial presence on their large, forested piece of land. It was a very fortuitous situation that I marvel at to this day.

The land had been on the market for many years (nearly the entire time we were living there). Because of this, it was always a possibility that it could be sold, and we might be asked to leave at any moment. Having said that, many years passed without that happening, so I had become pretty comfortable and relaxed about such a possibility. The land might never sell, for all I knew.

This morning, upon hearing the voices of two men laughing outside, I hopped out of bed, threw on some clothes and went to greet these unexpected intruders. I wanted to know what they were up to and assert my presence as the owner of the cabin. The men were both in their fifties and quite friendly when I said hello and introduced myself. One of them introduced himself as the person who had just bought the land we were standing on, and the other explained that he was the man who would be demolishing my cabin in the very near future. He followed this with a sincere apology, saying that it was a shame my home had to be destroyed, but that this was the exact site where a new house was going to be constructed as soon as possible.

"You've got a neat little place here," he commented, "but you only have about a week to clear out before we bring in the machines and tear it down."

I did the best I could to hide my complete shock and overwhelm, politely assuring the two of them that I would be out of there as soon as possible, and offering my congratulations to the new owner.

When I went back into the cabin, Preet was still half asleep in bed. I told her what had just happened, and she felt the best thing to do would be to cuddle and kiss for a while, which we went ahead with.

Later that day when I visited Kevin and told him what had happened, his assessment was much more stark.

"This is bad Miles, very bad," he said with a sense of deep concern, before launching into a battery of questions about my night with Preet. I told him that I'd shared all of my feelings with Preet, and she'd been very receptive. I explained that after sharing openly, we ended up spending the night together. Kevin was shocked by this.

"Really?" he asked in disbelief. "Your energy doesn't look like you've had sex at all. I almost don't believe you, but I know you're not lying. It's just that there's almost always a distinct glow from someone who has just had sex. It's very apparent in the way it nourishes and lifts someone's energy, but you have almost the opposite thing going on in your energy right now. How did it feel sleeping together? How do you feel after it?"

I hadn't yet had time to reflect on this, but I shared that it had felt nice, though there were still feelings of separation, distance and discomfort with Preet that hadn't changed at all.

Now that I was reflecting on it, being intimate with her felt like it may have intensified those feelings in some ways.

"Okay, give me a second," Kevin said, closing his eyes and taking a few deep breaths over several moments of silence. "Here's what has happened: You made an innocent mistake last night, but it has thrown your energy off in an extreme way. There was something emotionally unsafe about your experience with Preet. Your heart and your vulnerability did not feel safe with her. They actually felt the opposite. On these levels she was totally unsafe, and that's something you've felt over the entire course of your interactions. You guys had a nice conversation about the part of you that hasn't felt comfortable around her last night, but it didn't change that fundamental issue. It might have opened things up a flicker, but overall, nothing budged in a meaningful way. When you slept with her, you opened yourself fully to this unsafe dynamic. Her unprocessed wounds, the subterranean pain and anger she carries, you literally absorbed it, because you dropped your boundaries with her entirely. Because of your specific vulnerabilities and wounds, this part of her energy is like a toxic allergen for you, even though on the surface she's a lovely, kind and intelligent young woman." He paused to take another deep breath and examine everything before continuing.

"Energetically, you dropped your boundaries, then your heart was overwhelmed and crushed by a harsh foreign energy. And so that's what showed up this morning. A guy arrived to tell you he will literally be demolishing your home. Last night you did that to yourself, emotionally."

I was not fully buying this. How could just sleeping with someone, even if there were things about it that didn't feel emotionally safe or comfortable, lead to this? Surely the land had already been sold, and this turn of events was in place well before I made my choice to spend the night with Preet. When I voiced these thoughts to Kevin, he shook his head.

"You still don't get it," he said. "None of this would be happening if you hadn't shattered your heart last night. Your reality instantaneously changed in response to the choices you made and what they've done to your energy. If you had chosen differently, your reality would be completely different. If you had noticed how you weren't comfortable enough with Preet to invite her into your bed, I am certain those men wouldn't have been at your doorstep this morning, and you wouldn't be getting evicted. Reality is flexible and responsive, and arranges itself to meet you where you are."

This was consistent with Kevin's overall worldview, which I was slowly beginning to understand. Perhaps the most confusing thing for me to accept about all of this, however, was the notion that my sleeping with someone could be so emotionally devastating, and throw my energy into such extreme disrepair, that it caused this disaster. It seemed like such a normal thing to do, after all. I'd simply had sex with a person who I wasn't completely comfortable with. That is standard behaviour for most of humanity.

"Apparently you're extremely sensitive in this area," Kevin said. "There's no question what's going on here, though," he continued. "It is kind of surprising how extreme it is, but you're clearly on quite a unique path. Obviously not everyone reacts in this dramatic of a way to other people's energy. But on the bright side, if this is what happens when you sleep with someone really wrong for you, imagine what will happen when you sleep with someone really right?"

As we continued to talk, Kevin felt there was some good news: "This situation is definitely reversible. You do not have to lose your house. If you correct things as soon as possible, that won't happen. I can tell you this with complete certainty. But you need to cleanse your energy and your home immediately. You need to go home, tell Preet to leave, and aggressively clear your energy. Open every window, meditate, scream, smash things, scrub the floors, play loud music on your guitar. I don't care how you do it, you just need to completely reclaim your body and home as sanctuaries for your personal energy. Acknowledge everything that didn't feel good about your experience last night, everything you're carrying residually from it. Let yourself own all of these feelings, and celebrate the purity in you that has been so affected by this encounter. Affirm your separateness from Preet's energy. Completely reclaim who you are, the purity of your heart and soul."

After offering these instructions, Kevin urged me to get going, insisting this was all very time-sensitive. I found it difficult to tell Preet that she was no longer welcome at my place, but she was incredibly understanding, kind and gracious. I put her in touch with a friend who she could stay with, and then proceeded to open the windows of my cabin and decided to get some cleaning done. That felt like as good a way to cleanse things as any - I approached it as a kind of ceremonious, energetic exercise, breathing deeply and letting go of the emotional hangover I was carrying while sweeping the floor, doing dishes and scrubbing countertops.

Shortly after beginning this ceremonial cleaning, I started to feel very sick. My body was suddenly overcome with fatigue, achiness, and the onset of a fever that put me in bed, immobilized, for the following couple of days. I was so weak and tired during this time that all I remember doing was walking across the cabin to get some water and going to the bathroom in between long stretches of fitful sleep, cold sweats, and feverish, hallucinatory states of semi-consciousness.

When my health returned, I wondered if I'd gotten an STI (when I was later tested, this turned out to not be the case).

72

Kevin felt certain, however, that this was just my body processing the energy I'd taken on.

"You probably took Preet's energy on so deeply because you two slept in the same bed," he commented. "You drop all boundaries when you sleep, so in a certain sense it can be more vulnerable than sex. The fact that your sensitivity seems to be really opening up, and you don't know how to have healthy boundaries with that yet, also probably makes you more vulnerable."

In the days and weeks after Preet left, I felt like I was conducting somewhat of an experiment by seeing if my imminent eviction notice was actually reversible, as Kevin had contended. His advice to me during this time was that I would be able to stay at my place as long as I wanted to, with one condition: "You just have to be perfect, Miles. I mean, you need to manage your emotions and energy extremely well. If you don't, and you suffer some kind of implosion on that level like you did with Preet, the bulldozers will probably show up at your doorstep immediately. But now that you've corrected things and cleaned up your energy, there's no way you'll have to leave your home, so long as you are impeccable in the way you take care of yourself going forward. Again, you just have to be perfect."

Perfection, it turned out, is not my specialty. After about a month of spending most of my time alone in the woods (during which there was a complete absence of any further activity related to my supposed eviction and displacement), I went into town one evening to visit with some old friends that were passing through. Over the course of the night I had a few beers, something I wasn't accustomed to at the time. When I got home after this socialization and drinking, I was emotionally upside down. Both the alcohol and the company of my old pals had left me feeling deeply disoriented and depressed. I went to bed in a swirl of negative emotion.

The following morning, I woke up to the roar of heavy machinery and chainsaws in the forest outside my cabin. The excavators had arrived, and my time in the woods had come to a sudden end. Although Kevin had felt this eviction was preventable or reversible (he even saw one possible future where I was given the land I'd been living on outright), in a way I was happy and relieved to move on. After quickly grabbing the few belongings I'd prepared for a sudden evacuation, I said goodbye to my cabin and slipped into the forest, content to move on from a chapter of my life.

Chapter Six

For quite some time after I left the woods, I had no real idea what to do with myself or who I was now that I'd left my old life behind. My sense of self was shaken, and for several years to follow, it only seemed to unravel further. I had previously been an extremely confident, self-assured individual who was living with a clear sense of purpose, as part of a community of others who valued and respected that. Now, suddenly I was out of that role, wondering who I was beyond it, and growing increasingly aware that there were some parts of myself I didn't understand that were seeking attention, parts that I still didn't quite see or comprehend.

During this time, Kevin seemed to offer little help in navigating my existential drift. We began speaking less frequently, and he would often be evasive or unclear when I tried to understand what my next steps should be.

"You need to burn," he would sometimes say. "There are parts of you that need to be humbled. They need to be totally seen and owned. You must understand how they function and what they cost you."

This kind of advice generally just confused me further. It felt like he was talking vaguely about something I couldn't see, pointing out parts of me which acted like a vapour that would disperse if I looked in their direction.

When I expressed this genuine confusion to Kevin, he would say something to the effect of: "Miles, you carry a hatred in you that is absolutely terrifying. It literally feels like the hate of a white supremacist skinhead. It's that menacing, that intimidating, that cut off from empathy and grace, that caught up in its own pain and projection. You've allowed this energy to run your life, and you need to see how it smothers and destroys pure, tender vulnerability."

This was my diagnosis, and though I was no longer in denial around it, I had no idea what to do with it. Kevin never could offer a simple technique or modality for me to work with because he didn't believe in such things. Or maybe it would be truer to say that he felt they couldn't contain what he was holding.

"There is no modality for truth," he would say. "What you need is to develop a direct relationship with truth for yourself, and bring that into all parts of yourself, which includes the most vicious, hurt, innocent, immoral, and confused parts. There's no technique or method for that, it's just building a deep connection to truth."

To be completely honest, this advice went straight over my head, and I had absolutely no idea what to do with it. Because of this, for many months I more or less languished in a state of depression, feeling there was something deeply, fundamentally wrong with me, and clueless as to what could be done about it.

During this period I began studying a variety of teachings and literature that seemed adjacent to what I'd been learning from Kevin. I had a phase of devouring Carl Jung's work, other contemporary psychotherapeutic material, as well as a variety of new age, self-help and spiritual thought. My reading would often bring up questions to ask Kevin, and he would generally dismiss whatever teaching or modality I brought up as a distraction.

"It's your personal relationship with truth that matters, Miles. Can these books help or support you in developing that? Sure, maybe a couple of them can. But it's an actual relationship to the energy of truth in your body that you need to cultivate. You need to learn how to feel when your heart is closed, and then how to move from that closed heart towards an open heart. You need to develop an accountability inside yourself to truth, love and light, which are all different words for the same thing."

I understood what Kevin was saying at a certain level, but would often still be a bit annoyed by what I felt was an impractical, Zen master approach.

On one occasion, I asked Kevin why after spending so long learning from him, he'd never suggested meditation as a beneficial practice for me. His response was very memorable and emblematic of his philosophy in general: "Miles, I never stop meditating. I am constantly studying my energy, feeling what is happening in me, and grounding myself back into the present, back into my body and my truth. I'm constantly aware of how my energy is reacting to what is happening moment to moment, how I'm opening or closing my heart, feeling connected to or disconnected from truth, and the various voices - shame, fear, joy, neediness and so on - present in my awareness. That's what meditation is, and it should never, ever stop."

At the time, that sounded absolutely exhausting to me, like a constant micromanaging of one's internal world. But now, many years later, I understand the brilliance of what he was saying, and how the never-ending meditation he described is actually more natural and organic than the disconnection, pretending and disassociation one might consider a more normal state of being in our society.

As I continued with my educational reading and the occasional check-in with Kevin, the writer in me started stirring, and I came up with the idea of writing a book about what I'd been learning during this recent phase of my life. The thought of this was incredibly exciting - I'd be able to take my love for communicating and share some of the things I was now passionate about.

After a week or two of building up a concept for a book, I met with Kevin to ask him for his feelings on the matter. When I shared my process, his response surprised me. He told me that he'd been expecting this conversation for months, and was dreading it that whole time.

He explained that he didn't want to rain on my parade, but felt very strongly that the direction I was heading in did not feel good to him. "You need to do whatever you decide is in truth for yourself," he said, "but I have to be honest about the energy I feel and see. And what I see is that from where you are right now, the book you would write doesn't contain a certain light, and it won't take your life in a certain direction that I'll call your higher truth. It actually feels like you writing a book at this point would be a total diversion and distraction from you really making contact with your emotional body, humbling yourself, and getting into your heart. I'm not saying you couldn't write a successful book at this moment, but it's like you'd just be another mediocre self-help author who has a very limited, superficial level of self-awareness and understanding. That's fine if it's what you choose, it's a totally valid path, but I personally don't want to have anything to do with it. It actually sickens me."

As Kevin shared these observations, I sat and listened in a state of disbelief. This was not at all what I'd been expecting, especially given that the last time I'd told Kevin about a book idea I had, he'd been over the top in his excitement and support. His reaction now was completely different.

"Let me be very clear," he continued, "this is just who I am. I live for something much more penetrating and honest, and that's the higher path I see for you. It involves going much further and deeper into yourself, and it will eventually lead to creating something infinitely more profound. But it's not an easy path. It's certainly not a path that will give you instant gratification. In fact, it's the opposite - instead of soothing and boosting your ego, you'll be bringing its pain and insecurity sharply into focus and burning in that. Almost nobody wants to do this, and you don't have to, but I'm personally not interested in anything else. Again, if you choose to write the book you're talking about now, that's a valid choice - I just can't support it and want nothing to do with it whatsoever."

As I absorbed everything Kevin was saying, I felt my hope and inspiration being crushed by someone whose perspective I valued, and I didn't like it. A debate ensued, where I tried to argue for my ability and readiness to create a book, and Kevin countered everything I said with various versions of: "You can do whatever you want, I'm just holding a higher path." A part of me was indignant and felt that Kevin was being unfair in his assessment, which I told him repeatedly in a number of exasperated ways.

"Miles, do you know that you're triggered right now?" Kevin asked.

My voice had gotten deeper, my body was filled with tension and a burning sensation, my jaw was tight, and if I had retractable claws they probably would have been fully extended, ready to tear flesh to pieces. I paused in silence at his question, not sure whether I knew how to answer. Was I triggered? Or was I just reacting appropriately given the situation?

"Miles, this is why I'm telling you that writing a book at this moment doesn't feel good to me. There are some massive lessons for you to learn that are right here, in your face, and I think it would be crazy to do anything other than seize the incredible opportunity that's present in your life and dive deep into them. What's happening in this moment is a case in point: You're completely triggered, and you don't have any awareness or humility around it. You see me as a bad guy standing in your way. You see yourself as a victim of some oppression right now, and I'm going to be completely honest with you: You're batshit crazy. I'm your friend. I have your back. My energy is gentle and pure towards you. But because you've been hurt before, and because a big man was unfair to you in the past, a wounded part of you is re-experiencing its pain and projecting that onto me."

I had nothing to say in response.

"I'm your friend here, Miles. But listen to me again: You have more to learn, you haven't developed your own relationship with truth yet. Could you write a book? Sure. Would it be successful? It might be really successful. And that success might act like an extraordinary drug for your ego and fuel your most obnoxious, closed-hearted tendencies. But there's another path, and I can see it crystal clear: It's the path where you learn to go into your pain and your heart and really step into your truth. I'm not trying to convince you or stop you from doing anything, though. You should do whatever you feel is right. But at this moment, the energy with you writing a book is obvious. It's not on the pure, sacred truth level - not even close - so I can't support it. The moment that changes, however, I'll be your biggest supporter in the world."

I had mixed feelings about all of this. One part of me was impatient and annoyed at how Kevin made everything so complicated. Another part had faith in what he was holding, and was deeply curious to walk further along that path and to see where it may lead.

"You might not like this now," he continued, "but I'm doing you the biggest favour ever by sharing what I'm sharing.

Taking the time to do your inner work is going to make whatever you write in the future infinitely greater."

After this conversation, I reluctantly decided to put my book idea on hold for the time being, with feelings of disappointment, anger, and resentment stewing inside me. The part of me that just wanted to experience life and success felt held back and thwarted by Kevin, even though it was my own choice to not move forward with writing.

There had always been something slightly adversarial about my relationship with Kevin, but at this point that dynamic grew by leaps and bounds. Around now was when most individuals would have tended to exit Kevin's life, if they had even made it this far. He was too challenging toward people's egos and too triggering. I watched many friends, acquaintances, and strangers remove themselves from Kevin's life because he was so uncomfortably honest with them about their shadow (the disowned, unconscious parts of themselves). He would point out people's imbalanced egos whenever they surfaced, and sometimes in a way that actually inflamed whatever was already coming up. Kevin then became the bad guy, a know-it-all guru whose very name would trigger individuals into a defensive, agitated state.

I suppose anyone who sees and unabashedly speaks truth to the lies and inconsistencies of those around them will bruise a few egos along the way - Kevin did it with such boldness and gusto that he more or less left a trail of screaming egos in his wake. The fact that he had his own ongoing struggles and personal issues probably helped cast an additional shadow of doubt and distrust over him, as well.

Over time, people who'd fallen out with Kevin often seemed to come around and appreciate the harsh truth he had delivered and thank him retroactively. But in the heat of the moment, that was rarely ever the case. At this point in our relationship, I found myself on the fence, sometimes leaning towards the side of resentment, distrust, and vilification of Kevin, sometimes leaning to the side of humility and acceptance of what he was holding. The one time that I came closest to actually rejecting him and walking away from our connection completely, however, I was stopped in my tracks.

I had recently moved to Vancouver and was working at a small cafe while I got my bearings in a new city. Feeling good about the change of scenery and a fresh start somewhere different, I decided I'd had enough of Kevin's guidance. One evening I spoke with an old friend about the book I'd wanted to write, and how Kevin had felt it was something he couldn't support in any way. By the end of this conversation I had decided, with the encouragement of my friend, that it was time to ignore Kevin's oppressive influence and step out to forge my own path. A part of me just wanted to create, to share with the world what was exciting and profound to me, and felt more than ready to get started.

The following morning I was feeling very excited, thinking about my new trajectory and the book I was soon going to write as I rode my bike to work. It felt amazing to have a meaningful direction again, and the cold, crisp morning seemed particularly beautiful given my renewed sense of purpose.

My bike ride to work was all steeply downhill, and I was coasting at a high speed when an SUV driving toward me took a surprise left hand turn out of the blue, crossing the street seemingly at random and barreling into me. I saw what was happening only a split second before we collided, and thought to myself: "This is it, it's over."

In an instant, I was flipped off my bike and slammed against the vehicle's windshield, with one of my shoulders taking most of the impact. Splayed across the front of the SUV, I slowly realized I wasn't dead or unconscious. My right arm had somehow gotten stuck inside the little gap between the base of the windshield and the vehicle's hood, but aside from that, I seemed okay.

While I awkwardly extracted my arm from the vehicle's innards, the driver stepped out, looking like he might fall over from a heart attack at any moment, he was so overwhelmed.

He was an elderly man, probably in his mid-seventies, and was wearing a Catholic priest's uniform, black robe, white collar and all. I realized we were in front of a Catholic church, and he had been rushing there to deliver the morning service. Old ladies from his congregation soon gathered around, asking what was happening.

Unlike the last time I'd been hit by an elderly driver, I restrained myself from unloading all the profanities I knew at this terrified priest. He was clearly shaken - for a moment he seriously thought he had just killed a young man in front of his own church. He could barely speak and was trembling uncontrollably as we acknowledged one another.

I was honestly less upset than the priest. More than anything, I was confused as to why this had happened in the first place. I'd adopted Kevin's way of seeing reality as a reflection of my energy at this point in time, looking at notable experiences like this often as something intelligent and meaningful. Because of this, I found myself deeply curious what the meaning of this accident happening right now might be? I thought I'd just stepped back onto the right track with writing a new book and all, but here I was having a close brush with death on the roadside once again, and with a priest of all people behind the wheel.

After a few minutes of sitting on the sidewalk and establishing that I wasn't severely injured (the same could not be said for my bike), the priest offered me a ride to the hospital for an examination. I opened the passenger's side door of his SUV, still puzzled by why this was all happening, and noticed something quite striking: There was a tourist brochure on the passenger's seat, which I had to pick up and move out of the way, for the small town Kevin was living in. I immediately had a gut sense that the question I'd been asking, about why this had happened, was being answered. It had something to do with Kevin.

When I spoke to Kevin about the accident, he probed into what was going on in my life, which eventually led to me sharing my decision to go ahead and write a book. For him, that decision and this accident were completely linked.

"I generally don't like priests very much, Miles," he said, "but let's just say that immediately after deciding to go forward with this book, you were stopped by a holy man. Then inside his vehicle you stumbled upon a brochure that could have only been a clearer connection to me if it actually had my name on it."

I didn't fully understand Kevin's interpretation of this event, so asked him to clarify what he was saying: "You decided to go ahead on a path I warned you wasn't really in truth. Immediately thereafter, you were struck down by a priest - an emissary of divinity - because your energy was so out of alignment with truth. It's the same reason you got hit by a car when you were in that toxic relationship, and the same reason I knew it would happen. In both cases you were severely out of alignment with your truth. And in both cases you weren't supposed to die, just get shook. But believe me, if you continue on this path you've recently decided on, it's not gonna be pretty. Trust me, I'm as sure of what I'm feeling as I have been of anything."

I didn't necessarily disagree with Kevin's interpretation of this event, but I didn't like it, and part of me wanted to be free from this teacher/disciple relationship I'd found myself in.

Near the end of our conversation, Kevin floated the idea of the two of us working on a book together, and him getting fifty percent of the earnings. I would write under a pseudonym (to keep my ego from getting inflated), and he would remain anonymous. The part of me that was distrustful and wary of him, however, wanted nothing to do with this. That part of me felt as though Kevin wanted to take away my creative process, freedom and money. Kevin saw us collaborating as a great opportunity for me to learn, and in retrospect it was, but I was too frustrated and fixated on my desire for independence to appreciate that at the time.

The following day, I was still stewing in angst around all of this when I heard a knock on the door of my little basement apartment. It was the police, looking for my neighbour Joe. I told them they had the wrong door, and that I didn't think Joe was home. Curious if there might be some kind of meaning to the cops showing up, I asked them what was going on, which they informed me they weren't at liberty to share.

My neighbour, Joe, was a well-meaning guy, but not a very pleasant person to live next to. He actually managed to fulfill most of the duties of a stereotypically bad neighbour, regularly making loud noise late into the night, not responding to requests to be quieter, leaving a mess in common spaces, and so on. He was always very kind when we interacted face to face, but he wasn't an ideal neighbour.

When I heard him getting home later that afternoon, I popped out to say hello and ask what the police had been coming around for. He explained that he'd gotten a little out of control with his ex-girlfriend recently and began behaving in a way that basically amounted to stalking her. As a result of this, she had filed a restraining order against him, and the police wanted to speak with him about this.

According to Joe, his ex-girlfriend had a nefarious spiritual teacher that was controlling her life. This teacher was a highly questionable person, according to Joe (whose opinion itself was highly questionable). He claimed that the teacher was behind her choice to break up with him (a decision that actually sounded pretty solid from my perspective). "The worst part," Joe explained, "is that now this so-called teacher wants to take fifty percent of whatever money she earns doing her own spiritual work with people, because he's supposedly mentoring her. It's totally insane!"

Joe felt he needed to help his ex see that she was on the wrong path and win her back. In the process, he admitted that he had gotten a bit carried away, obsessive, controlling and creepy, though he didn't share any of the details or specifics regarding how that played out with me.

At this point, I realized that I may be witnessing a miraculous reflection of my own stupidity. I suspected that Kevin would say my impassioned and misguided neighbour was a brilliant reflection of me. His out of control anger over an unfair spiritual teacher wanting some kind of fifty percent split of financial profits was a literal match to my current situation. And it was clear to me that my neighbour was absolutely in the wrong as he described his circumstance. He was acting from a place of highly charged emotion, disconnected from what would be healthy, respectful or appropriate in his situation.

It was tempting to see my neighbour and his situation as a confirmation that I was being taken advantage of by my own spiritual teacher. But as I listened to Joe describe everything, it was blatantly obvious that his ex-girlfriend's mentor was almost certainly a better influence in her life than he was. I sincerely liked Joe on many levels, but the way he spoke about his ex and the entire situation was disturbingly closed-minded, obnoxious and controlling. There was no doubt in my mind that I would have told his ex to run for the hills from him if she'd asked me. This led me to believe that I was seeing my own out of control fear, distrust and closed-mindedness being mirrored back to me.

Chapter Six

When I shared this all with Kevin, he felt it was completely unsurprising. "This is what I've been telling you, Miles. The part of you that is stubbornly triggered by me right now is not seeing life clearly, and totally lacks humility around it, just like your neighbour. There's nothing new here, and the fact that it's showing up for you to see clearly outside of yourself in this way is textbook. You are exactly like your neighbour currently. And, as you might be starting to realize, it's not a good look."

This incident was a bit of a turning point. In its wake I decided to drop all intentions of writing a book. I also chose to challenge my feelings of resentment and frustration towards Kevin, and instead turn towards the darkness he was pointing out within me, and see what might come of it.

As I began to focus on all the things Kevin had been illuminating, I once again asked him what exactly it was that I needed to do to move forward on the path he was suggesting. And again, he continued to give answers that seemed incredibly vague.

"You need to learn how to feel like shit," he said on many occasions. Presumably he meant that I needed to learn how to feel the emotion I'd disowned (and was often simmering in, consequently) and accept it, instead of continuing to ignore it. When I asked him what that might entail practically, he continued to sound more like a confounding Zen master than a practical life coach.

"You'll need to burn in hell for a while. You need to really feel your shame, to honestly see what you've become to avoid your vulnerability, and then get underneath all of that to feel what is at your core. Parts of you will absolutely hate this, they will fight it as though their life depends on not being seen or felt."

As I mentioned earlier, Kevin did not practice any particular method or modality of working with emotions and energy. "There is no modality for truth, Miles," he would often say. My work was to develop a direct relationship to the parts of my being that were rooted in truth - that is, rooted in something deeper than the traumas, conditioning, and petty grievances I carried on the surface. To develop a relationship with what it felt like when I was connected to that truth, and what it felt like when I was coming from my wounds or conditioning, and create a bridge between these two aspects of consciousness within myself.

"Truth is an energy, Miles. Being familiar with what that energy feels like is how I do what I do. I can feel when something is in truth, and I can feel when something is not. I'm constantly studying the energy of myself and others, testing to see if it is in truth or not. You're filled with voices that have no regard for truth, that feel totally separate and distinct from truth. You need to study these voices, feel the differences in their energy, and then make bridges in your awareness between all the disparate parts of yourself and the truth that burns beneath them."

That sounded absolutely mind-boggling.

"The trick is," Kevin continued, "you currently believe most of these wounded, non-truth voices. They make up a substantial part of your personality, who you think you are and the identity you feel you need to defend. You'll need to let that go, and that's not easy."

This prescription felt murky. Just burn in hell? Learn how to feel like shit? Create a bridge between 'the truth' and my wounds? Whatever this all meant, I figured I'd give it a try. With a renewed sense of determination, I left my job at the cafe and decided to live off of some meagre savings while I turned away from the world and all distractions to see if I could crack into the mystery Kevin had been pointing to. For much of the summer that followed, I spent my days in a strict regimen of inner work.

Practically speaking, this looked like shutting the blinds of my little basement apartment every morning to block out the sunlight and warmth of the outside world, as I lay down on the floor or sit upright, eyes closed, and attempt to simply start feeling. My intention was to just let go and see what would come up in that empty space, then let it all wash over me - to let all that I'd disowned and suppressed come back to the surface, one feeling at a time.

The most actionable advice Kevin gave me in this endeavour was the following: "Give your feelings a voice. Whatever you are feeling, just give it a voice, let it speak through you. Don't ever censor it, but don't always believe it either. You're just tapping into raw emotion or energy, and allowing it to move and discharge by letting it speak. It might have some very twisted beliefs and incorrect perceptions of reality, but what it feels underneath all of that is real."

I had watched Kevin process his emotions and energy on countless occasions, often 'giving it a voice' exactly as he had instructed me to do. Because of this, I had a bit of an idea what he meant and what could be expected, though doing it still felt like walking out into the dark without a flashlight or any sense of the landscape before me.

My initial efforts were blocked by my own resistance. On the first day of this experiment, all I felt was a blankness and numbness. There was no great eruption of feeling, no profound emotional fireworks or cleansing as I usually witnessed flow easily when Kevin worked on himself. There was just a wall, nothing to report but blank, numb space.

I lay in silence with this wall for a long time, waiting expectantly for something to happen, until eventually I decided to try giving the wall itself a voice. Kevin had said give whatever I felt a voice, after all, and presumably numbness was included in this. So I felt into my numbness and started saying: "I'm numb. I don't feel anything. I'm blank. I don't *want* to feel... anything. I don't want to feel. I don't want to feel at all. I don't want to feel... sad. I don't want to feel my sadness..." And suddenly the wall collapsed, and I burst into tears.

I sobbed and sobbed, continuing to give a voice to the feelings as they changed and evolved, as numbness gave way to heaving emotion, voicing whatever was present in each moment.

"I'm ready to feel now," I said aloud in the empty room, my face and shirt drenched with tears.

The primary feeling I uncovered during this session was sadness, and a lot of it. I wasn't sure what this sadness was from, but the very notion that I was actually there, ready and willing to feel whatever was inside myself, was itself deeply moving to a part of me. When I said out loud that I was 'ready to feel now,' it was as though an incredibly lonely child was receiving the attention he'd been waiting for his whole life, and tears gushed out of him. Eventually I felt too exhausted to carry on, as though I'd emptied a tank of all it contained for the time being, and got up to go to the bathroom.

When I told Kevin about this experience, he was very supportive and encouraging, telling me to continue with what I was doing and that it was exactly what was needed.

As I continued, most of the time what I felt when I sat or lay down to 'process' was a thrashing rage, anger, and even hatred. I'd lay down, and almost as soon as I started focusing inward and searching to give a voice to whatever feeling arose, my body would start clenching, jerking and convulsing, and I'd be voicing feelings through a clenched jaw in a deep, vicious growl. A typical transcript of one of these sessions would look something like this: "I'm angry! I'm so angry!

AHHHH! Fuck! Fuck! FUCK!" Some variation of these words would be repeated over and over.

This would go on for an hour or more sometimes, my body thrashing as jolts of energy shot through it, fists clenched, stomach tight, face red. I had no idea if what I was doing was correct, but there was definitely something intense and raw in me that I was tapping into.

After a few days of this, I remember my whole upper body aching like I'd been in a gruelling military boot camp. Just going for a walk was painful, my muscles were so incredibly tender and sore after thrashing intensely with these feelings of anger and rage.

Much of the time there was no story connected to the emotion or energy that came up during these early inner work sessions, or not that I was consciously aware of at least. I was seemingly just feeling raw anger and rage. Occasionally it felt connected to my father or another family member, an ex-girlfriend or an incident or relationship from my past. But more often it was just a lot of violent thrashing and intense vocalization. I often wondered if my neighbours could hear me, and if so, what they thought. I'm sure I sounded absolutely insane, spending warm sunny days thrashing around alone in a dark room, furiously repeating statements like: "Fuck everything! Fuck everything! I'm so fucking angry!"

Although I felt like I must be making some kind of progress, it's probably worth noting that I wasn't actually feeling all that great during this period. In fact, I felt pretty awful a lot of the time, but I thought that was the prescription I'd been given, so continued on with my season in hell.

When I checked in with Kevin after a short hiatus in our connection, however, he had some surprising observations. "Your energy feels incredibly toxic, Miles," he said. "It's like you've just been dredging up all the toxicity in yourself, then swimming in it, and dredging up some more. You're not holding truth or light for these wounded parts of yourself, which is the whole point of doing inner work. You only go into these hurt parts to hold them, to understand them, educate them, nurture them, and show them truth and love. Otherwise you're just getting drowned in your own negativity and toxicity. There is benefit in you simply owning and feeling these feelings, but I think you've just been festering in them."

These details were news to me, and I felt like it would've been helpful to have heard about them at the beginning of the summer, but either way, the message was now being received.

"It's great that you've made contact with all of this pain, anger and sadness. That's huge," Kevin continued. "But now you have to take care of these parts of yourself. Enter into a nurturing dynamic with them. Give them the support and love they should have received long ago."

For a moment I was frustrated that I'd possibly wasted a considerable amount of time and energy torturing myself alone in a dark room due to my inexperience and ignorance. But this little piece of information turned out to be of such significance, that it was worth whatever missteps led to it. It wasn't enough to just visit and stir up my pain, I needed to do something to take care of it. I needed to protect, educate, validate and love it. In Kevin's words, I needed to hold truth for it.

Around the time of this conversation, Kevin and I began speaking more frequently, sometimes for hours a day. Kevin was focusing intensely on his own inner work at the time, as his chronic illness continued to cause him constant pain, and he suspected that his unresolved emotional wounds were at the core of it. He always preferred to do emotional work with someone else present, even if they were just on the other end of a phone call silently witnessing him. He felt that his energy was more grounded by another's presence, and the work felt more tangible and powerful to him if it was witnessed by someone besides himself.

Thus began a period of me silently listening to Kevin while he did emotional work on himself that lasted for many years. During this time, it would not be unusual to spend several hours a day on the phone with Kevin as he processed childhood traumas related to his family, grief and hurt from botched partnerships or overwhelming life experiences, as well as general undercurrents of shame and insecurity that had coloured his entire life.

Kevin was very much the archetypal wounded healer. His capability to empathically understand and hold space for others amazed me constantly, but there was no hiding the fact that he himself was a man deeply in process. In fact, I had never (and still have never) met anyone so completely upfront about their own wounds and blocks. And yet he was simultaneously the strongest, wisest person I'd ever crossed paths with. It's probably safe to say that those two things (his open vulnerability, and deep wisdom) were related.

I knew that I was receiving a gift during this time: I was diving headfirst into working on myself, and simultaneously getting to participate in a daily routine of sitting in on a very skillful individual working deeply on himself. Usually Kevin would add a side commentary as he excavated and processed his energy and emotions, periodically letting me know exactly what he was doing, and why, to make it all the more educational for me. Because he was so acutely aware of energy, he was measuring everything he did in a very direct way, feeling when parts of him were shifting and responding either positively or negatively to his interventions (he was also able to assess and comment on my inner work from an energetic perspective, which was incredibly valuable).

I got to see how he excavated different feelings, gave them a voice, allowed them to shift, then gave them a corrective experience either by strongly protecting them, ferociously validating their innate goodness, or educating them like a divine big brother. Sometimes he would go back to where an emotional wound originated (an experience of being bullied as a child, for example) and take care of the hurt part of himself back there, providing the nurturance and support it hadn't received at the time.

The way that he could feel and relate to all of the energy and emotion within himself was truly remarkable to witness. He would feel specific parts of himself trapped in overwhelm, enter into a dialogue with them, and watch as they softened and their energy transformed through his caring, protection, love and attention.

Since Kevin refused to distill anything down to a modality or technique, I instead got to learn in an incredibly organic way, by simply hanging around, watching and listening to someone at work with themselves. I was rarely taking actual notes, but the simple fact that I was around this activity so much meant some things slowly began to rub off on me. It might not be a fair comparison, but I've often looked back at this time as something akin to a musician learning how to play improvisational jazz by hanging around other more advanced players jamming together. I imagine an individual listening, soaking things in, asking questions, and eventually developing their own ability to freely explore the craft without a bunch of theory being taught, but instead by absorbing the discipline through an organic process. That's what happened over the time that I was sitting in on Kevin's inner work.

The fact that Kevin was a wounded healer was in some ways a blessing for me, because I got to see him work on some of the exact same wounds I contained. Sometimes, after listening to him process trapped emotions related to his childhood and father, he would say to me: "Miles, everything I was just working on directly applies to you. In fact, you could actually cut and paste all that I was just processing onto you and your stuff, word for word. It's identical." I was bearing witness to exactly what I needed to do. My wounds were seemingly very similar to Kevin's (I learned during this period that our fathers even shared the same name - Ken - a coincidence that seemed to reinforce how similar some deep parts of us were). And because Kevin's issues and personality were somewhat complex and difficult for him to shift, I was able to witness this inner work over a long stretch of time - long enough that I couldn't help but gain an understanding of the general dynamics of all that I was observing.

Kevin remarked on several occasions that it was almost like this was set up to be the perfect education for me. Either way, it was an incredible experience, and what I learned through it proved extremely valuable as I continued to engage in the excavation of my own heart.

Chapter Seven

"Can you try to open your heart, Miles?" This is a question that Kevin would often ask me at the beginning of our conversations, and one that I often had no idea what to do with. He would regularly call me up wanting to explore some feelings he was looking at from a new angle, or a life situation he was navigating. Before we could get to any of that, however, he would need me to open up so that he could feel comfortable and at ease in my presence. I could only be helpful to him if my energy wasn't closed or dysfunctional. On many occasions, this led to a lengthy exploration of my heart and what was keeping it closed. Because of this, Kevin's stuff would frequently never end up being discussed at all. And, on many of these occasions, my heart didn't actually open up at all. Instead, I would be left with some type of homework to focus on or sit with by myself.

To be honest, for a long time I had absolutely no idea what Kevin meant by "open up your heart". Did he mean think happy thoughts? Suppress whatever inhibitions I had? Pretend to be loving and kind? I didn't know. And often when he asked me to open my heart, I thought it already was open, though the question itself provoked my insecurity and defensiveness (which probably closed my heart off a bit more than it already was).

Because Kevin could feel my energy (and the energy of my heart), he could feel how open or closed I was, and would let me know if I was on the right track or not during these conversations, moment to moment. To him, an open heart was not a theoretical concept or an abstract ideal, it was something incredibly tangible and concrete, as measurable and palpable as the shifting temperature of a room. The open heart could be felt, and it was accompanied by a whole different way of thinking, perceiving, relating to others and holding oneself. It was a distinct state of consciousness.

Still, I usually felt lost when he said: "Your heart's closed right now Miles. Can you try to get into it and open it up?" If I didn't even know my heart was closed in the first place, how would I know what opening it meant or looked like practically? It all felt very nebulous and intangible to me.

When I explained this to Kevin, he responded by saying: "That's because you're used to being disconnected from your heart. You need to begin studying yourself and the energy of your heart. Pay attention to when you feel connected to it, and when it's slammed shut. By doing this you can start to develop reference points for when your heart actually cracks open a little bit, so you know what that feels like. One reference point that you already have for an open heart is when you are in love with a woman. That's a place where you very much open your heart, albeit in a narrow and immature way."

I asked Kevin to explain what he meant by "narrow and immature" here.

"You can open your heart and love in the confines of one little corner of your life, with a safe person, in a bubble," he replied. "You can actually open up quite a bit within that safe little bubble, and simultaneously remain closed and callous to the rest of the world. In fact, to whoever is outside of that tiny bubble, your heart is generally closed. That's not how mature love or a healthy heart function. That's the limited bandwidth you've been operating on, but it's just a tiny fragment of what is really available and natural. A heart that reserves itself for only the safest, softest, most inviting moments of life is a heart that lacks courage, depth, strength, and wisdom. Still, there is a reference point for you in your experience with romantic love. You'll know how it feels to have an open heart if you remember what you feel in such moments."

Another reference point I had for what an open heart felt like, that was even clearer than romantic love, was being alone in nature. Kevin again both acknowledged and criticized this sanctuary of mine: "You can open your heart when you're alone in the woods because there's nothing there to challenge you," he said. "There's no fear of judgement, no one to trigger your shame, insecurity, competitiveness, lying and pretending. There's no one to hide from, no one to make you feel lonely or incomplete. So you can just expand and be you. It's safe to let go of any posturing or shrinking, and actually relax into what's natural and true to yourself. And of course that feels amazing, that's why you fixated on that experience for so long and spent a lot of time alone in the woods, because you have no idea how to feel that sense of openness and grace in the world."

Indeed, the best I had ever felt in my life, the most connected to myself, free from fear or insecurity and in ecstatic love with the beauty of life, was after extended time alone in nature.

"But again," Kevin continued, "this just illustrates your pattern of chronically closing your heart. As soon as you come back to people and human relationships, your heart shuts down. You don't know how to hold yourself open in the complexity of the world. It would take real courage, real honesty with yourself and others to live with an open heart amid the chaos, but a long time ago you learned to habitually close off instead of being bravely open. You've gotten so used to being closed that it's just normal at this point. What you need to do is learn how to be that natural, free, loving person you've been while alone in the woods, but in this chaotic world with all its contradictory energy."

This was all true, though I'd never looked at myself and my life in this way. As I sat and absorbed what he was saying, another question came to mind: What do I do? Where do I even begin if I want to change this?

Kevin suggested I develop a regular practice of watching myself, and my heart, as I go about my days: "Observe what comes up when you interact with people. See where your heart goes. Notice when you feel compassion, shame, disgust, competitiveness, vanity, anger or insecurity. Watch the ways in which your heart opens and closes in response to others, and ask yourself why that is happening. If you are really honest with yourself, you should be embarrassed by much of what you see."

With this homework laid out clearly, I began a daily practice of watching myself as I walked down busy city streets and quiet forest trails, when I went to get groceries, engaged in conversation, or any other time I had some kind of proximity to or interaction with another human.

One of the first things I noticed when I started this was a part of myself, a part I usually ignored and tried to pretend wasn't there, that wanted energy and attention from nearly every woman I crossed paths with. This part was like an inexhaustible void that yearned for female energy to suck up. It felt needy, impulsive, and weak. And, if I were to use Kevin's terminology, my heart was almost certainly not open when I felt this compulsive neediness. Though I felt attraction and desired the attention of women while in this dynamic, I didn't feel a sense of openness or empathy toward them at all. I felt slimy and weird, like I was playing a game or acting, and insatiably grasping for a very superficial sense of approval and acceptance. I didn't feel natural, comfortable with myself or confident in who I was. I actually felt a deep sense of being incomplete, like the women I was fixating on had something I desperately needed. It was a pretty bleak thing to witness and to own.

Things only got worse when a woman was with a man. I almost always had a competitive part of myself that came up in this scenario. This part of me had no empathy for the man. They were just a competitor for female energy and attention, not a complex human with all the vulnerability, innocence, and sanctity that implies. I could feel my desperation for love and attention driving my lack of empathy for men who might stand in its way, and behind that, a deep lack of respect for myself. And all of this while casually strolling down the sidewalk to get some groceries.

The idea of constantly paying attention to these subterranean emotional dynamics seemed overwhelming. Was it healthy, or even possible to be aware of this stuff all the time? Kevin definitely thought so.

"Not only is it possible," he explained, "it's what actually being a sane and conscious person looks like, Miles. You've buried and disassociated from these parts of yourself because they were painful and shameful to look at, acknowledge and accept. The problem is, they'll never get to evolve or heal if you keep them hidden in the underground of your psyche forever. There are very specific reasons you feel compelled to grasp for attention and energy in this way. There's an ocean of insecurity and pain behind it. And if you don't face the monsters you've got inside yourself, you'll never heal the pain they are trying to protect. You'll never get your real self back, and you'll never get to show these wounded parts of you the truth. There is part of you that believes life on earth is absolutely ruthless and unfair, nothing more than a series of betrayals, disappointments, and soul-crushing rejections that one must be guarded against. Part of you actually fully believes that! And it basically runs your life from behind the scenes. Of course it's totally wrong, and just seeing reality through the lens of its unresolved trauma and hurt. You have the opportunity to show it that. You have the opportunity to bring these hurt parts of yourself to heaven, literally. You can show them that life is fair, beautiful, sacred and intelligent. You can show them what you've been learning since you met me: That there is an intelligence behind everything that happens in this world. Hardships and failures are actually sacred lessons. Life is loving, life is beautiful, you deserve all the love in the world, and you never have to close your heart to receive it. Love is not a scarce resource you need to push and shove others out of the way to get at, there is always enough for everyone. It's an infinite, unlimited resource. You never, ever have to close down or manipulate to receive it - that actually makes you cut your heart off from love, which starves your wounded parts from what they really want at the deepest level. It is literally the most counterintuitive thing you could possibly do."

With this, my homework became an ongoing assignment: Watch my meanness, my insatiable ego, my vanity, my shame, my competitiveness, and the insecurity that drives them as I move through my days. Attempt to pause these impulses, understand the deeper workings and motivations behind them, and then show them a bigger picture of life and love. Most importantly, see if I can find pathways to an open heart through all of this. Then report back to Kevin for regular briefings.

When Daniel came to visit me during this time, I received an embarrassingly clear view into one of the closed-hearted dynamics of mine I'd been starting to catch glimpses of here and there. Daniel was briefly passing through the city, and stayed at my place for just one night. We met up and went out for sushi together early in the evening, then took a long meandering walk around the city and talked for several hours before returning to my apartment, where Daniel set up his sleeping bag on the floor beside my bed.

As we were getting ready for sleep, Daniel spoke to his new girlfriend on the phone. I hadn't met this romantic interest of his yet, so at one point during their chat he put her on speaker phone so that I could introduce myself. All in all, nothing of great significance seemed to have happened over the course of the night, until we talked about it the following morning.

Over breakfast, I told Daniel about some of what I'd been working on with Kevin - studying the hidden, hurt, insecure and insatiable parts of myself. I described the part of me I'd observed that endlessly sought attention and energy from women, that was competitive and closed-hearted, and could see other men as mere competitors for the endless attention it wanted. I felt somewhat proud of my growing self-awareness, until Daniel brought me back to the ground.

"Were you watching that part of yourself last night?" he asked.

I didn't know what he was talking about, so asked him to explain. He shared that the previous night when we were out at the sushi restaurant together, he had felt something in me change. We were being served by an attractive young woman, and he felt me close off to him whenever she came by, as I engaged in some kind of game or act, clearly trying to draw her attention towards me (and away from him).

"To be honest, I think you were doing some version of what you just described with me throughout most of the night. While we were walking through the streets, I could feel you change whenever we passed by young women. It's like you became a different person, and would totally close off to me. And then when I was talking to my girlfriend, that was the most obvious. Were you aware of anything that you were doing when I put her on speaker phone and introduced you to her?"

I stumbled for words and felt shame burning in my veins - I'd suddenly been put in the hot seat, caught red-handed. I hadn't been paying attention to these dynamics when Daniel and I were out and about, but he had been, and having it all come out into the open this way was a shock to my system. Seeing my shadow in the bubble of meditation or during solitary introspection was one thing, but talking about it openly within the real-time motions of a friendship was much more difficult. Having it seen clearly by another person felt almost paralyzingly embarrassing.

Daniel was actually more curious than upset, though. He was wondering if I'd been doing this subtle manipulation - shutting down my empathy to him and clamouring for attention from women - throughout our entire friendship. He felt that might help explain some of the intense insecurity he often felt around me. We had been friends since I was a kid, and for most of that time Daniel's insecurities had kept him from exploring any kind of romantic or intimate relationship whatsoever. He wondered if having a best friend who was emotionally unsafe - throwing him under the bus to gain all the attention his greedy, insatiable ego could get its mischievous hands on - might have fed into his tenuous sense of self-confidence.

There was an extended silence as I burned in shame. Once I let myself go back and look at the events of the previous evening honestly, it became clear that what Daniel was pointing at was true. I had wanted that waitresses' attention. I had stopped fully seeing and treating Daniel with integrity during that time. I'd stopped having compassion for him. There was something about me that tightened up and closed off - it was insecure, it was needy, it felt that love is a scarce resource it needs to rush and push others over to secure. When he was talking on the phone with his girlfriend, I had felt the same impulse. Again, the insatiable part of me was awakened, and it wanted attention, it wanted female energy. It felt a part of Daniel's girlfriend that was open, that could feed its hunger, and in my brief interaction with her, I played with that. In that brief interaction, Daniel's humanity once again faded from my consciousness, and all that mattered was the sexual energy of the woman present. That this woman was Daniel's partner seemed unimportant to this needy part of me (or maybe made her even more alluring, as it could step in and gain the attention of another man's woman, proving its worth and desirability in an incredibly shallow, sad way).

Daniel had felt it all, being a very sensitive and perceptive man, and it had overwhelmed him. He froze and shrunk, as he'd done throughout our entire friendship, trying to ignore what he was feeling, and becoming confused about what exactly was going on, wondering if maybe this was nothing more than his own insecurities and projections being stirred.

I wasn't entirely sure what to say. This was my best friend, and I'd just been caught vying for attention from his girlfriend. What could be sleazier? And at the same time, it could be argued that all of this was happening at a subtle, energetic level. I hadn't actually done anything - I hadn't actually gone and physically had an affair with his lover or even overtly flirted with her. So was any of it real? Was it worthy of the shame I was burning in? When Kevin weighed in, his answer was an unequivocal yes.

"Energy is real, Miles," he said. "What you are doing with your energy is affecting everything and everyone around you, even if they're not fully conscious of it. Daniel can feel it, the women can feel it, and that changes all of their behaviour. It also clearly changes your behaviour, even if only subtly.

Doesn't that make it real? This is one of your problems: You might think that because you don't usually do horrible things with this energy that it's okay. For example, on the surface you aren't an overt, manipulative womanizer, and in general you aren't stereotypically superficial or mean. So it would be easy for you to say: "I'm a good person on the surface, and that's all that most people see," and therefore let yourself off the hook and never own or take responsibility for all the pettiness and meanness active inside yourself. That would be a massive mistake though, because this energy is very real. It totally shapes your life, it owns you, and it keeps you from actually being open to love and connection. It does hurt people, it creates a trail of bruises and pain in its wake. It crushes tenderness, it terrifies vulnerability and beauty. All the things this wounded part of you longs to experience the most, it destroys. It's a living, active, energetic force, and it will rule you until you fully accept it and choose to relate to it differently."

In the case of Daniel, I feared that owning my shadow would mean losing a friend. Strangely, however, when I admitted that what he was seeing was all true, and that I wasn't entirely sure what to do about it, he felt more relieved than anything. Kevin remarked that this was because if I learned to be honest and clean with these parts of myself, "Daniel might actually get a friend he can trust."

There was something about this revelation that was bigger than I understood at the time: Hiding the needy, insecure, wounded parts of myself made me scary to be around. Bringing them into the open made me safer, even if it meant giving a voice to some really awful things (in this case, the awful thing sounded something like: I wanted your girlfriend to want me more than she wants you. Not because I'm actually interested in her, but because I'm wounded and act that out like a vampire). When I kept this stuff hidden, it operated unconsciously and caused mischief. When I brought it into the open, there was a possibility for something different, something honest and open, even if it was also awkward and confusing.

When we spoke about this, Kevin said: "Your situation with Daniel is perfect. Can't you feel how your heart closed while the two of you were at the restaurant? And when he was on the phone with his girlfriend? Don't you feel how you shut him out of your heart completely? You were no longer holding him with empathy as a close friend, you were seeing him as a rival. He was basically reduced to a hunk of meat to you, your consciousness had become so primal, brutish and barbaric. You must be able to feel what I'm talking about?"

I tried to put myself back in those moments, and as I did, it became clear to me what Kevin was speaking about.

"Miles, I want you to try and fully see Daniel. I want you to let yourself see the purity of his heart, to see how all of his dysfunction, insecurity and neuroses are caused by his immense tenderness and sensitivity. I want you to see him the way your soul sees him. Really, truly open your heart to Daniel. Can you do that?"

I tentatively said yes, and then Kevin waited in silence as I closed my eyes and fumbled around inside myself. As I began to focus inward, all I could feel was a blankness and a fear of doing this wrong in front of Kevin. He seemed to notice what was happening, and responded to it by quietly commenting: "Just let yourself feel the truth, Miles."

With my eyes closed, I pictured Daniel. I saw him sitting in my apartment as I flirted with his girlfriend over the phone. I saw his tender heart overwhelmed with all that was going on. Not striking out, not hating, not angry. His heart was as innocent as a child, and simply confused by the dishonest and mean egos around him, as a child would be. I began to cry.

"You're seeing it now," Kevin gently observed.

I found myself seeing many flashes of Daniel across our history of shared experiences, seeing his innocence, gentleness and overwhelm, as my sobbing continued. I was moved beyond words by all the love I felt for him.

"Now your heart is open Miles," Kevin stated. "This is what it feels like! Can you please take note of everything going on in you right now? Do you feel your empathy? Do you feel your gentleness? Your humility? The breadth of your perspective? This is what it feels like when your heart is open. You see through different eyes. You see a bigger picture of life. Now, from where you are in this moment, can you see more clearly how your heart was closed to Daniel when you two were together?"

I was still crying, but I managed to eke out a yes in response to Kevin's question.

"This is what life is supposed to feel like all the time, Miles. Where you are right now, heart open, able to see things from a bigger picture perspective with empathy and understanding, this is what we call normal from here onward. We need you crying every day now, that's mandatory."

This I didn't understand. Kevin thought that having an open heart was just how life was meant to be lived at all times, yet I felt like I would never stop crying if I stayed in a place of such rawness. I was still crying as I explained this to him.

"That's fine," he rebutted. "Then you'll be the beautiful guy that never stops crying. But in all likelihood, you'll probably just keep on crying until you're finished crying. And right now you have permission to take as long as you need with that. I'm watching something beautiful unfold, and it's an honour to witness it. Take your time."

As I mentioned already, the sense of shame I felt after owning my dynamic with Daniel was almost paralyzing. Kevin commented that I should be ashamed, that I should be burning in embarrassment, otherwise I wasn't seeing things clearly. The problem was, I found shame would often immobilize me and shut me down completely, making me want to crawl into a dark hole and languish alone in my ugliness, unworthiness and irredeemable awfulness. Following this incident with Daniel, Kevin could see what was happening with my shame, and offered some words of advice: "The key is to be able to clearly see and own all of the viciousness, pettiness and evil in you, while still maintaining a firm sense of your fundamental goodness. Miles, you *are* a lying, manipulative dirtbag. And you are *also* divine to the very core. If you can't hold both of these realities together, you've lost the plot. You can't actually hold your light in a grounded way unless you've owned your shadow. And you will not be able to bear owning your shadow if you don't have a firm connection to your divinity. At the moment you get totally overwhelmed and depressed by looking at your wounds because your connection to light, or to your heart, is so weak. The two must be developed together, or you won't have the resources to handle your pain."

This was certainly true for me - I spent long stretches of time overwhelmed by the reality of my closed-hearted tendencies, unable to see that while one part of me could be quite callous, manipulative and cruel, there was another deeper, more fundamental aspect of my being that gave my less admirable impulses context, and made holding them bearable.

One evening shortly after Daniel's visit, I laid down on my bed with the intention of exploring the part of myself that had been exposed during his stay. I closed my eyes, and as Kevin often suggested, searched for the energy or feeling present in me.

In my mind I went back to the moment when Daniel was talking to his girlfriend in my apartment, and let myself feel into the part of me that had desired her attraction and attention. I felt how weaselly and needy this part of me was. I felt its competitiveness, and decided to start asking it some questions, beginning with: "What do you really want?" What happened next surprised me.

Suddenly, in my mind's eye, I was on the wooden porch of the house my family lived in when I was four years old. My two brothers, my mother and I were there together, and I was filled with a deep desire for attention and love from my mom that I distinctly felt I wasn't receiving. I felt sad and left out, like my brothers and others were getting all of the love and attention I wanted. I was simultaneously feeling the frustration and sadness of my four-year-old self, and witnessing him separately from my adult awareness. There was no notable action or interaction going on between my family members and myself, just a profound sense of longing, rejection, and sadness.

Then, suddenly, I was in complete darkness. I felt warm, insulated, and comfortable. It felt like I was in salt water, or amniotic fluid. My surroundings were peaceful and gentle, and I was extremely calm. Then I became self-conscious. I suddenly felt incredibly ugly, as though I were a tiny, decrepit alien, totally disgusting to the very core. It felt as though there was something fundamentally wrong with me, that everything about me was ugly, gross, out of place and unloveable.

I became aware of voices, thoughts and feelings of others just beyond the walls of my little home. It was people. It was the people I was about to call my parents, and I could feel that they didn't want me. They were arguing about it. I panicked. "This must be a nightmare!" I thought. "This can't be happening! This can't be the reality I'm about to enter! They don't want me?" My tiny heart was totally devastated, totally overwhelmed. It seemed there had been some horrible mistake. My very existence, it would appear, was a horrible mistake. As I reacted to the voices arguing on the outside, I felt that I was a burden, that I must have some fundamental flaw, some horrible defect, and my little heart collapsed in on itself.

Again, I was feeling both the experience of this unborn fetus, as well as the perspective of the adult Miles bearing witness to his dilemma. Suddenly the fetus broke into uncontrollable tears, which I cried in my adult body, while laying on my bed. Though this little guy was absolutely devastated, the adult me felt nothing but complete awe and love for him, and was smiling and laughing that he could ever have believed he was a burden, it was so preposterous and far from the truth. Soon I found myself violently crying and deep belly laughing simultaneously. The love I felt for this little guy was instinctive, absolutely automatic and unquestioning. Without saying anything, I let him know that what he was feeling from his parents was just their confusion. They were basically children, afraid, confused, wounded and immature, consumed by their own personal dramas. The very idea that he was anything but a divine gift of the highest order was truly laughable. It was an absolutely absurd joke, his sanctity was so obvious.

I continued laughing and crying for a long time, and gradually the fetus transformed from a dark, alien looking creature that couldn't stand itself, into a healthy, calm baby boy surrounded by golden light, as I heaved his tears and held an instinctive love for him.

Eventually my crying tired itself out, and I returned to normal awareness in my bed. Whatever had been happening felt complete, as I opened my eyes and realized that I had to go to the bathroom.

Once I'd put myself together in the wake of this experience, I was eager to tell Kevin about it, curious what he might think or feel about its significance.

"It looks like you've made contact with the core of your insecurity, the part of you that feels totally rejected by life and love and carries a sense of deep unworthiness," Kevin observed. "Isn't it amazing what's actually behind your compulsion towards arrogance, hardness and vanity, if you're willing to sit with it, Miles?"

I thought about this for a moment before responding: "It seems like what's underneath those harsher parts of me is their complete opposite."

"Exactly! Your harshness, your alpha male tendencies, your emotional armouring, they're all so well-practiced and intense because of the enormous ocean of pain and vulnerability directly behind them. You have a tight, well-honed, defensive shield because you're the most tender, sensitive person in the room most of the time, and you have no idea how to hold that without feeling like you'll be destroyed. God knows there's a good reason for your insecurity. This part of you has every reason to feel betrayed and wounded because of his experiences in the past. That's not the problem. The issue is what you've been doing with those feelings unconsciously. You see how pausing to be with them, rather than compulsively acting out your old pattern with them, can take you to light and into your heart? Can you see that this wound is either your ticket to heaven or hell? Every time it gets triggered, every day as you move through life with this inheritance, you get to choose: Love or shame? Truth or non-truth? Will I own these feelings and do something conscious, courageous and beautiful with them, or will I disown them again and have them overtake me like a drug? Will I get drunk and stoned on my fear and insecurity, acting out to overcompensate for them? Or will I face these feelings with clear eyes, and discover a natural high on the other side of them? Will I let my insecurity harden me, or soften me? Make me unkind and brittle, or compassionate and wise? Are you finally starting to understand what I'm talking about here?"

For the first time, I very tentatively felt that I might be.

Chapter Eight

The number of times that Kevin kicked me out of his life were far too vast for me to keep count of. The first occasion where this happened was probably a year or so into our relationship. At the time, he felt that my tendency to get triggered in his presence and transform into an angry curmudgeon was becoming too burdensome to be around. In his words, my energy was just too dense for him. He very gently, kindly, but firmly told me we wouldn't be able to speak or hang out with one another anymore, with one small caveat: He said that this was an invitation for me to change. He made it clear that if I were to sincerely own and work on the patterns he was reacting to within me, he would happily welcome me back into his life. Until then, however, it was farewell. Kevin felt that he was doing me a massive favour by removing me from his life, framing it as an opportunity to witness how my unbalanced ego and closed heart were causing me to lose out on good things in life (in this instance, him).

When this initial disconnection took place, it was somewhat devastating for me. I felt like an awful person, rejected because I was simply too messed up to be tolerated. There was a positive side to this turn of events, though. I also felt deeply humbled and driven to work on myself like never before. And without someone else's wisdom to lean on, I started to focus more actively on accessing my own.

Kevin and I didn't just break up that once, however. A similar scenario repeated itself countless times over many years, as Kevin would always end up resuming our connection. Sometimes it would take a couple of days, sometimes weeks, and at most a month or two (I would've had to have done something really serious for such a long separation to hold), but I would always receive a phone call out of the blue at some point. Kevin would have decided there was a matter he wanted my perspective on, or he needed someone to listen while he processed something that had come up. Or maybe he was just bored and wanted a person to talk with. Regardless of such details, our disconnections were frequent and generally short-lived. After a while it became a bit of a joke. When I would tell Daniel that Kevin and I weren't talking anymore again, we would both just laugh and shake our heads, knowing how many times this had happened before.

During one of our longer breaks, I met and started dating a young woman named Tanisha. Tanisha was a very spiritual person, a quality that I found quite attractive about her, but also somewhat confusing. Her spirituality was confusing for me because a lot of what she believed in and practiced, although I wanted to support and understand it, made a part of me reflexively cringe. She often casually spoke of seeing aliens and angels, engaging in certain shamanic rituals, and a variety of other esoteric perceptions and practices. Often when she did so, I found myself seizing up in discomfort. I found myself deeply questioning and judging her beliefs, and I didn't like that reaction in me. I felt consistently thrown off and uncomfortable when she spoke about her spirituality, as though some alarm was going off uncontrollably in my gut. I didn't feel comfortable with this automatic, visceral response, so I more or less buried it, and did my best to be superficially amiable, polite, and kind. Occasionally, I would gently challenge a statement or belief Tanisha expressed that felt very shaky or questionable to me, but by and large I took the role of passive kindness, suffocating the part of me that was constantly discerning, feeling and questioning.

Tanisha and I had great chemistry in many ways, and I loved how open and expressive she was with her thoughts and beliefs, but there was something that also felt like it didn't quite click from the beginning of our time together. I couldn't see our relationship developing into a long-term, serious life partnership. It felt more like sharing joy and fun together for the time being, and I communicated this on many occasions. Tanisha, however, was more open to something serious developing, which I did my best to be honest and gracious around.

Just over a month into us dating, I got overwhelmed by a squeamish feeling that had been growing in me since the beginning of our connection, and decided there was no sense in prolonging a situation where the two of us wanted very different things. With as much love and respect as I could hold, I told Tanisha that it felt best for us to stop seeing each other, and that was the end of our connection.

A day or two after having that talk with Tanisha, Kevin called me up out of the blue to chat (unceremoniously ending our latest disconnection). When I told him in detail about the experience I'd just had with Tanisha, his assessment of my behaviour was surprisingly brutal. I thought I'd done a pretty good job of being honest about my intentions and feelings from the very beginning of my brief connection with Tanisha, and that I'd been very respectful throughout our entire experience together. Kevin disagreed.

"Miles, you really dropped the ball this time," he said. "You withheld your truth to a disturbing degree, and it made you so uncomfortable and anxious that you had to run for the hills just so you could breathe."

I wasn't quite following, so asked Kevin to explain what he was seeing more clearly.

"Every time Tanisha talked about some aspect of her spirituality or beliefs that you felt was ungrounded, you withheld your feelings. And withholding in this way is just a polite way of lying. Instead of being honest about your perceptions, your feelings and your discernments, you were a little weasel, sneaking around, pretending to be unconditionally nice and loveable. You weren't actually being honest about who you are and what you felt, and so she had no opportunity to see the actual person she was spending time with and decide if she wanted to be with him. Instead, she got the guy you were pretending to be. Do you see what I'm talking about?"

I sheepishly said yes.

"How would you rate your honesty with Tanisha in the area of beliefs and spirituality on a scale of ten? How honest were you?"

I thought for a few moments before answering: "Maybe a six?"

"I think you're being generous with that assessment. But either way, you get a horrible grade. I mean this is basic stuff, if you aren't completely honest with strong feelings, you'll probably end up exploding or hitting the emergency eject button on the relationship sooner or later. You chose the latter. I think you were legitimately reacting to things in Tanisha that were ungrounded and unhealthy, and you chose to bottle that all up. Then, eventually your withholding was too uncomfortable, and you chose to run away instead of giving your truth a voice. Given all this, can you see why I think you totally failed to show up and to hold your truth in this connection?"

Again, I reluctantly said yes.

"The discomfort of your chronic dishonesty is why you ended it. You didn't walk away for a legitimate reason, you walked away because of your hiding and lying. If you had shown up, were totally honest, and she wasn't into you, that's another story. But we can't have that conversation, because you chose to hide. You don't even know what kind of chemistry you two actually have, because you didn't experience a fully authentic interaction together."

I should have known I had this coming. The entirety of Kevin's philosophy could be distilled down to one word: Truth. He was belligerently committed to truth, both in the sense of being nakedly honest, and in making choices that are aligned with one's personal truth. I had committed a massive betrayal of truth throughout my entire connection with Tanisha - burying my thoughts, feelings and authenticity because I didn't want to challenge her, upset her or be rejected by her. I was afraid of someone not liking me or getting mad at me for sharing honestly. I was afraid of coming across as arrogant or judgemental for questioning someone else's thoughts and beliefs. But I didn't actually have a choice, my energy reacted to certain things whether my brain wanted it to or not.

Kevin's thoughts on my relationship with Tanisha didn't end here, though: "It's important to recognize who you become when you don't share your truth. Can you see how withdrawn, angsty, frustrated, and edgy you became with Tanisha? Can you see how your heart had to shut down to her because you weren't honouring yourself by sharing honestly? Tanisha started to feel oppressive to you, when she had done absolutely nothing wrong. The only crime she committed was being herself. You're the one who buried your truth. You're the one who disowned and betrayed your feelings, and so of course a very deep part of you felt anxious and oppressed. But that part of you mistakenly felt that this was Tanisha's fault. You became closed-hearted, frustrated and distant, and you blamed Tanisha for those feelings when it was all self-inflicted. Miles, this is very important: If you would just be honest with your feelings all the time, you'd stop feeling like a victim, you'd stop turning angsty, and stop being an asshole with a closed heart to people who don't deserve that. When you stop collapsing around others, you'll stop needing to get defensive and frustrated towards them."

I had indeed become frustrated with Tanisha during our connection, and even when I told Kevin about my experience with her, there was a subtle harshness, irritation and disdain in the way I spoke about her. Kevin saw this as me unfairly blaming an innocent bystander for my own negligence and dishonesty.

"Imagine you'd never shut down with Tanisha, Miles. Imagine you'd held your truth around her since the moment you two met. What would have been possible? My guess is that even though you may have challenged a lot of what she shared with you, she probably would have liked you even more than she already did. That kind of honesty is a rare and precious gift to receive from a person. And you would have been able to feel comfortable and natural with her, because you respected yourself. Instead, you did what every cowardly, emotionally disconnected guy does - you pretended to not have deep perceptions, feelings and needs. Then you went numb when those disowned feelings started twisting in your gut, and eventually ran for the hills when all that energy and emotion was too uncomfortable to bear. An opportunity was squandered."

Although his assessment was pretty severe, Kevin didn't feel that all was lost. He strongly felt that I should apologize to Tanisha, own how I hadn't shown up authentically in our connection, and share everything that felt significant which I'd previously withheld from her. This sounded painfully awkward, but it wasn't the first time Kevin had encouraged me to initiate such a confession. At Kevin's insistence, I forced myself to reach out to Tanisha, who was wide open to meeting up and talking.

Telling someone you previously dated that you withheld and misrepresented yourself to them in massive ways is not usually a fun conversation to have. I suppose it could have been worse - I wasn't confessing to an infidelity or obvious superficial betrayal of trust, although at a deeper level, I actually was. The person Tanisha developed a connection with was not the real Miles - it was part of him, but I'd kept some very vital aspects of him hidden, misrepresenting myself and misleading her. I had to admit that there were countless times I'd felt a strong aversion to, or even a repulsion from, some of her spiritual beliefs and practices, but I had been too scared to share my feelings. I had to own that some of this was probably related to my own baggage and insecurity. But it also felt like there were some things that I was having a healthy, natural, legitimate reaction to - things that felt like unprocessed trauma and ego wrapped in spiritual clothing. Things that felt ungrounded, and that I didn't trust. I didn't like admitting to my feelings, but a deep part of me was consistently reacting in a strong way when these matters came up.

When the two of us met, I tried to share this all in a non-judgemental, gracious way, because at the end of the day, I didn't think I knew any better than Tanisha. I just wanted to be honest with what I felt and make that okay to talk about. Given how difficult and awkward it was for me to share all of this, despite my best efforts and intentions, my delivery was more or less a total disaster.

Looking back on this conversation, I still feel bad for Tanisha. She was clearly confused and hurt by all of the things I was bringing up. She couldn't understand why I was sharing this stuff with her now. Was I just trying to hurt her? I'd already broken up with her, why was I coming back to tell her a bunch of additional bad stuff? Was this some twisted, sadistic, manipulative thing I got off on? She felt judged, confused, and angry. I knew that was totally fair and understandable, and as things continued to unravel over the course of our conversation, I began to suspect I was at the helm of a complete train wreck.

I explained to Tanisha that my intention was to actually show up and respect her in a way I hadn't previously, to show her who I honestly was beyond my hiding, and see if that would create a new path where it felt good and made sense for us to be in each other's lives.

Her reaction was exactly what I feared: She got extremely defensive and angry, yelling at me until I had to just apologize for everything and end the conversation to avoid further catastrophe. I then received a number of furious text messages accusing me of being sadistic, abusive, and cruel.

Kevin was a bit surprised by Tanisha's reaction, but conceded that I'd built our whole connection from a skewed foundation, so it was understandable. "You withheld your truth from the beginning with her, so you trained her to think you're a person that you aren't. To suddenly bring your truth out this far into the connection in a jarring way, is a messy situation. If you'd been real and truthful from the beginning, you two either would have gotten together in a more healthy way, or you would have butted heads immediately and went on your separate paths. She may have been able to receive your truth if it wasn't totally shocking and contradicting a bunch of other behaviour."

We both agreed that either way, it was good for me to have made an awkward attempt at correcting things. Not because I wanted a girlfriend out of this situation, and definitely not because I wanted to cause any harm to Tanisha, but because it was a lesson I needed to learn, and the painful experience of messing up and having to go back to try and fix things retroactively, only to have my ass handed to me, helped emblazon it in my mind. And though I felt bad for causing Tanisha more hurt and confusion, it also felt good that she got to know the truth about me, mostly so she could understand that she'd been dating a coward, and perhaps feel a bit of peace in herself with that bit of information.

I was less surprised than Kevin by Tanisha's angry reaction. One of the reasons I'd held back my honesty so much with her was that, from the moment we met, I felt a very strong, unhinged anger and defensiveness in her. This didn't excuse my hiding or withholding in any way, but it did play a role in it. As I was learning to understand and trust my energetic impressions of others, Tanisha's reaction was a validation of something I'd very clearly felt.

After discussing the overall lessons of this situation, Kevin offered one final thought: "If you're just honest in the first place, everything is a lot easier."

Chapter Nine

A few months after my experience with Tanisha, I met another young woman named Tara. Tara and I had actually been introduced to one another a few years earlier through mutual friends, and happened to cross paths again, as we were now living in the same area.

I was speaking with Kevin daily at this time, so when Tara and I went on a first date, I knew that I'd be talking to him about it afterwards (the two of us openly shared the details of our love lives with each other). With this awareness, there was a sense of accountability - I would have to do things differently, or suffer Kevin's disappointment and criticism once again. I definitely didn't want to go through another disastrous confessional conversation after being inauthentic with someone, so I prepared myself to act more honestly.

Tara and I met for tea on a cold spring afternoon, and although I tried my best to pretend that everything was normal as we got into a conversation, I felt as though I had a thousand eyes watching my every move, seeing if I was going to show up and be real or not this time around. There was a sense of needing to get it right that stifled my ability to be natural and at ease in the moment - I was studying my every thought, word, and action, hoping to catch myself when I slipped into lying, withholding or disowning my feelings.

Tara and I spent a couple of hours talking, at first in a cafe, then walking on a path along the ocean, sharing parts of our past and present as the conversation flowed. During this entire time, I felt a painful disconnect between the two of us. Tara had launched into a steady stream of talking the moment we met and shook hands, and hadn't yet paused long enough for either of us to feel what was going on, filling up all the space with very heady talk. I was yearning for a break in the conversation, a space to breathe and get a sense of what was going on inside myself and between us, but we seemed to have gotten on a track of seamless, cerebral, emotionally disconnected conversation.

After years of having Kevin in my life, this was both painful and strange. Conversations with Kevin were always about what was happening emotionally and energetically in the moment. Long breaks of silence facilitated this kind of relating, and I'd become accustomed to them. On this date, not only had we failed to pause and connect to our energy or feelings even once, it felt like the conversation was actually being used to actively avoid doing that, maybe because it could potentially be vulnerable.

I recognized that my lesson here, if I were to push myself and be completely honest, was to share with Tara how disconnected our whole interaction was feeling. Once I'd put this all together, I waited for the first semblance of a break in conversation, and asked Tara if I could share something that felt difficult to admit. She was wide open, and I explained that over the course of our brief time together that afternoon, I hadn't been able to feel much of anything, because we had only been interacting from our heads in a very cerebral, superficial way.

I explained that this was very uncomfortable, and a bit frustrating, because I sincerely wanted to know if the two of us had any chemistry, but it felt like there was a wall up preventing me from getting any sense of that. This wall was blocking any real possibility of connection, and though I appreciated our conversation on a certain level, there was something extremely stifling about it. It felt like we weren't actually getting to know one another in a real way at all.

Tara was completely open to everything I shared. She acknowledged the dynamic I spoke of, and admitted that she had a habit of filling up space with speech to avoid the vulnerability and discomfort that empty space might lead to. It was a protective mechanism, a way of feeling in control, smart, and safe. She deeply appreciated me bringing this up, and shared that it was a habit she wanted to change, but had no idea how to go about doing so.

Neither did I, but I wondered if instead of pretending it was normal to have a massive wall between us, maybe just acknowledging the wall could point to a way through it.

The sky was getting dark by now, so we walked to another cafe, sat down across from one another, and both went somewhat blank. A lengthy silence ensued, during which the wall between us did not magically disappear, but instead seemed to come awkwardly into focus. There was still a feeling of discomfort and disconnection between us, only now we were painfully aware of it. Tara seemed to be avoiding talking entirely, afraid that anything she might say could further entrench the sense of separation we were experiencing.

Then, in our protracted blankness, I got inspired to tell Tara why I even wanted to see if we had chemistry - it was because I had a vision of a deeply connected, loving relationship, and I saw her as a possible partner.

I was about to go into this, but my shyness and insecurity stopped me after a few words. Tara pushed and prodded me to continue, until I realized I had no choice but to share: I explained that the type of relationship I wanted to experience was like a therapeutic experience for both people, where they could learn to be completely honest and authentic, to reveal their deepest vulnerabilities and insecurities in a safe and healing context, to give and receive support, love, and understanding to and from the purest parts of each other. I delivered a passionate monologue about what my heart really yearned for, but before I was able to finish, I began to choke on my words. I noticed that Tara's face had turned a deep red, and my heart felt like it was going to explode with a thousand ecstatic butterflies.

"What's going on for you, Tara?" I asked. "Did your heart open up?"

I'd spent enough time with Kevin at this point to have a clear sense of when someone's heart was open or closed, and it felt like Tara's heart had just had a dam removed from it, allowing a reservoir of pent up love to crash out beyond its restraint.

She said that it felt like the wall we'd been talking about was completely gone - her heart felt totally, ecstatically open, as though she was high on an extraordinary drug. I felt extremely high too, and for the next ten minutes or so we sat beside each other like a couple of drunken teenagers, giggling and speechless as waves of euphoria washed over and through us. We looked into each other's eyes in total amazement, as though non-verbally asking each other "Are you feeling what I'm feeling!?" and breaking into uncontrollable laughter in sync with one another. It seemed that we were mutually experiencing a blissful altered state, simultaneously feeling strong rushes or waves of energy rise and fall as we sat together. I would try to form sentences and say something about what was happening, but the feeling of bliss was too much, my words would fall apart as I began to speak them, and I'd fall back into euphoric giggles. There was nothing I could say or do, the feeling of love was completely overwhelming.

Eventually Tara realized she had a dinner she was supposed to get to, so we collected ourselves somewhat, exchanged a hug and said goodbye. We were both very much looking forward to a second date.

Later that night when I spoke to Kevin and told him about my experience with Tara, he felt that it was exactly what one should expect if they are being truly honest and vulnerable.

"This should be your new normal, Miles," he said. "Really, that level of honesty is something you should never turn off, and it will lead you to bliss and connection like you've never experienced. Look at how extremely different your experience today was from your experience with Tanisha. In both cases something was making you squirm inside and it was difficult to share, but in this case you actually did it. You challenged yourself and owned your feelings. And not only did that let you breathe and feel comfortable, it made real connection possible. So congratulations, you deserve what you got to experience with Tara today. I'll be curious to see where things go next!"

I was curious, too. Before ending this conversation with Kevin, I asked him if there was anything else he wanted to share.

"There's definitely something here," he responded, "just give me a second to look at it."

After a moment of silence and a few deep breaths, he was ready to speak: "Something is going on energetically that I think I need to acknowledge. It's what your energy is doing relative to Tara - something is going on in you that just isn't sitting right. I wasn't going to say anything, but it's so strong and uncomfortable that I think at the very least I need to ask you if you're aware of anything that feels off?"

I had no idea what Kevin was talking about, and told him that everything with Tara felt great to me.

"Okay," he continued, "that's what I thought. My suggestion to you then - and it feels like I'm being guided to tell you this in a very clear way - is to take some time to really feel out whether Tara is the kind of person you want to form an intimate connection with. There's something extremely weird happening with your energy when you two come together, and I would strongly encourage you to go into the energy yourself and feel into how you two do - and don't - match."

Kevin seemed to be throwing cold water on my amazing potential new relationship, and I found this thoroughly confusing. I reminded him of the incredible, ecstatic heart connection Tara and I had experienced, something I assumed was an obvious sign of extraordinary relationship chemistry and alignment.

"Miles," he replied, "you two have a resonance, and you were very honest with Tara in a way that opened both of your hearts. That's all that means. It doesn't mean you would be good partners or even good friends. People experience heart connections and resonances with each other all the time, then mistake that as some kind of soul mate or twin flame thing and romanticize it into something much more fantastic and fateful than what it actually is. The level of resonance you and Tara experienced is something that I feel with people all the time, and if they are somewhat open they will feel it too, exactly as you described. I have to explain to people regularly that this doesn't mean we are meant to be partners or lovers, it's just what it feels like when two souls really meet and exchange love. There's no deeper meaning to it than that."

We spoke at length, as I tried to understand what Kevin was saying, and work through my resistance to anything that might cast doubt on this exciting new connection. He patiently fielded every question I had, consistently reminding me that he was my friend, that he cared about me, and wasn't trying to stop me from having good things in my life.

"I'm not saying anything about how you should proceed with Tara, but there is something really strange and unsettling going on in your energy when you connect with her, and I would strongly encourage you to explore that for yourself. I feel very strongly about this Miles - what's coming up here is extremely important."

With Kevin's observations fully delivered, we ended our conversation, and I wondered to myself once again why everything had to be so complicated with him. I was honestly only aware of my enormous excitement and joy at the very real possibility of getting to connect with a beautiful, intelligent young woman. Even the subtle notion that something about this connection might be 'off' was triggering to a part of me, but the sincerity of Kevin's plea was enough to get me to explore whatever it was he was picking up on.

Later that night, I lay down on my bed and tried to look at my connection with Tara as clearly as possible before going to sleep. I closed my eyes and began to consciously feel into the emotions present in me. All I could sense initially was my excitement, desire, and impatience to connect with Tara again. Whatever 'off' feeling Kevin had been speaking about was not on my radar.

After a while, I began trying to look at things from Kevin's perspective, attempting to see what he was seeing, but that didn't feel helpful. It felt like I was trying to force myself to embrace someone else's perceptions without really having a clear sense of my own. I then tried to simply look at myself more objectively: If I suspended my desire, loneliness, and neediness, was Tara an appropriate person for me to bring into my life at a deep level? Did connecting with her really feel good and right to me? What did it do to my energy? I did my best to step beyond my yearning and look at everything from a more honest vantage point, but this approach didn't lead to any sense of clarity, either.

Then I decided to look at things from Tara's perspective. Not from her persona, with its desires and projections, but from her soul. I looked at what would actually give her soul what it needed in a relationship, the type of match that would truly meet her at a deep level and speak a common language with her heart. Immediately, everything was crystal clear. Not only did I feel that I wasn't this type of match for Tara, we felt miles apart on a subtle, emotional level. There was absolutely no question, I wasn't even close to being an ideal partner for her. And I felt no sense of disappointment, inadequacy or jealousy at not being such a person. It just felt like we were different in our emotional makeup and the way we approached life. I wanted Tara to experience the feeling of being really met in a partnership, and it felt very obvious she would not and could not experience that in certain ways with me. I actually felt that she would be perpetually unsatisfied in a relationship with me - not because of some inadequacy of mine, but because we simply didn't align with one another's needs at a basic level. We both contained depths the other would never quite understand, and had chambers of our hearts that didn't meet or connect in certain ways, and that was that.

As I felt into this, the intense longing and desire for Tara that had been buzzing in me calmed down and faded dramatically. The annoyance and confusion at what Kevin had been directing my attention towards also vanished. There was a sense of rightness, understanding, and acceptance in me. I didn't know what any of this meant relative to moving forward with Tara, but I fell asleep with a feeling of deep inner peace.

The following day I shared this process with Kevin, who said that everything I described lined up completely with what he had been feeling. "There's just something awkward, forced and unnatural about you two coming together," he shared. "I totally honour the way your hearts connected on that first date, and I think it was a huge gift for both of you. But beyond that, it doesn't feel like you two make any sense in a connection together."

After this process, I found myself in a confusing place of not knowing how to proceed with Tara. I'd felt a deep level where we really didn't match, but she was still an extremely beautiful, intelligent, and kind young woman who was open to me romantically. I wasn't sure what to do with all of this.

As it happened, Tara had her own internal shakeup in the days following our first date. For reasons that weren't entirely clear to me, she almost completely pulled back from being interested in connecting further. The level of vulnerability we had gone to so quickly may have felt scary and made a part of her close down, seeking the safety of a more controlled and familiar emotional landscape. Whatever the exact cause, when we spoke next it was clear that both of us had undergone some significant inner shift, and while we still shared a deep appreciation and respect for one another, there was a mutual desire to step back and not pursue a connection further. Because of this, that first ecstatic experience together turned out to be the full extent of our relationship. And though it was only a momentary glimpse of bliss, I was incredibly grateful for it.

Kevin moved to Vancouver a couple of years after I had done so. His decision to relocate was made rather suddenly one afternoon, when he felt the overwhelming need for a change of scenery and set his sights on Vancouver. With a sense of urgency and excitement, he decided to uproot himself and move before finding a place to rent, asking if he could stay with me while sorting out the details of his living situation. I was happy to host him, so for about a month Kevin relocated to my bachelor suite while he searched for a new place to call home in a new city.

Kevin's requirements for a suitable apartment were somewhat unique and specific: Aside from the usual details like location, size, and aesthetics, his environmental sensitivities meant that a suitable home could not have been recently constructed or renovated. Things like freshly painted walls, newly installed hardwood flooring, carpets and the like were all sources of subtle chemical scents, or 'off-gassing,' that would make him seriously ill. Because of this, if Kevin was interested in a place, he would have to go there and carefully smell it before it could be considered as an option.

While he was searching for a new home, Kevin and I shared my tiny, one-room apartment, setting up his sleeping bag on the floor beside my bed. To call this apartment tiny is probably being generous - Kevin took up much of the available floor space just by laying down on it. Aside from when one of us went to the bathroom, there was no privacy or personal space whatsoever. We were constantly around one another, and while he stayed with me I took on the role of a devoted helper more than that of friend or pupil. Every day we would go to look at new places, and I would constantly stress about things like women wearing strong perfume sitting beside us on the bus, which was something that could seriously trigger Kevin's chemical sensitivities and make him sick. I was hyper-aware of Kevin's disabilities, and was hyper-vigilant in trying to make sure he was protected and taken care of at all times. This meant running errands, carefully planning trips, and changing plans on a moment's notice if some possible danger arose. This consumed most of my energy for the duration of Kevin's stay with me.

Kevin appreciated my support, though he was much less concerned about any potential dangers or threats to his health than I was. He felt as though he was simply taken care of, that everything would invariably work out and there was no reason to get stressed about anything (in stark contrast to my anxiousness and worrying). He was also a bit like a kid in a candy store once he arrived in the city, and just wanted to enjoy himself in a new and fascinating environment. After living in a small town for years, being in a big metropolitan area with all of the novelties it contains put him in a mood to cut loose and explore.

Nearly every day he would take trips to the casino downtown to play poker, sometimes making over a thousand dollars in less than thirty minutes, sometimes losing almost as much in half that time. It was all very nerve-racking for me to watch. Because of this I would generally either wait outside the casino or just go home and let him have his fun.

For Kevin, poker was both a form of entertainment and an opportunity to flex his intuitive and intellectual sharpness. According to him, the secret to winning was simply managing his energy and studying the other players. If he was in a good state energetically and emotionally, and reading everyone at the table, victory was assured. What seemed to always throw him off was the problem of the casino itself being toxic. I mean this literally - artificial scents perfumed the entire place, no natural light got into the building, and the strong chemical fragrance of freshly installed, thick carpeting permeated the poorly ventilated rooms. He could handle about fifteen minutes of this chemical assault on his system before his body got overwhelmed and his energy began to crash. In that initial fifteen-minute window, he usually made a killing at the poker table. But then his excitement and desire for more action would keep him playing, while his head started to burn and his eyes turned red and glossy. Eventually he would realize he'd made the same mistake once again - he'd stayed too long, reacted to the chemical scents in the air, his energy had tanked, and he had either lost all of the money he won initially or much more.

Regardless, Kevin was beyond elated to simply experience life in the city, going shopping for new clothes, exploring various neighbourhoods and simply interacting with humanity. I, on the other hand, descended into a state of constant fear and anxiety, worrying about Kevin's well-being and overextending myself as a host. Kevin seemed so preoccupied that he didn't really notice or comment on this, and I seemed to think it was okay to temporarily feel awful given the exceptional circumstance of helping a friend out.

When Kevin eventually found an ideal apartment to move into, I helped him on moving day. We rented a van and I did the majority of the heavy physical work, making sure Kevin didn't exhaust or hurt himself (his illness compromised his capacity for physical exertion). After we had finished moving all of his belongings and setting up his new place, the two of us went for a walk downtown to celebrate his new home before parting ways. During our walk, I asked Kevin what he thought was the most important thing for me to be focusing on in my life at that moment. This question was born out of idle curiosity, more to make conversation than anything else. There was a long pause as Kevin closed his eyes and felt into what I'd asked, during which his mood shifted from being casual and light to something more contemplative and intense.

"You're still completely ruled by your shadow, Miles," he said. "Just look at the past few weeks of your life. Look at how you've handled having me stay with you. Your energy has been totally consumed by fear and worry this whole time. When was your heart open? When did you even peek out from beneath your veil of angst and frustration? Honestly, at your current pace, you'll be ruled by these old habits for the rest of your life. You are a prisoner, fully and completely, to your wounds."

Kevin was almost yelling at me as he shared these observations, offering a passionate, unfiltered assessment while we walked along a busy downtown sidewalk. I noticed a woman walking alongside us, watching our conversation with eyes wide open and a look of amusement across her face. I told Kevin that maybe we should find a more private place to talk, but he was actually emboldened by my discomfort, saying that he thought the woman beside us liked what she was seeing, before continuing.

"Miles, what you haven't yet understood or integrated is that you never, ever, have to feel the way you've been feeling for the past few weeks with me at your place. Really look back at how you've felt during this time. Your brooding frustration and anger, your lack of openness and honesty about all that you're going through. You should never, ever force yourself to endure that. Your heart has been slammed shut, and that's completely unnecessary. You wanted to support me, which is great, but you overextended yourself and stopped taking care of your needs in the process. You suppressed feelings of frustration, anxiety and fear, and your heart closed off as a result. You failed completely on this level - the level of talking things out as they come up and getting back to an open heart. Do you understand what I'm saying?"

I was somewhat in shock, having intended my initial question as nothing more than a trivial conversation starter, but I did understand. It was weird being put on blast by someone I'd just bent over backwards trying to help (and specifically for how I had gone about helping him). But it was true that for the entire time that Kevin was staying with me, I'd been in a state of anxiety, discomfort and fear, and instead of owning those feelings, talking them out and moving through them, I withheld them and proceeded in a constricted, closed-off state.

"You didn't need to help me with anything if it wasn't your truth, you know," Kevin added. "I would have been totally happy and supportive if you had decided it just didn't feel good to host me or help out with my move in any way. I trust that no one ever has to betray themselves for me or anyone else to get what they need in life. And there were a thousand times when you could have paused to say: "Kevin, I'm not sure if this feels good to me," or, "Kevin, I've got a lot of fear and resentment coming up that I'd like to work through, would it be okay for us to focus on that for a bit?" I would have been totally supportive of that. This entire experience, both the past few weeks and your life overall, can be whatever you want it to be. It can be a pristinely honest, beautiful, emotionally awakened work of art where you open your whole self to the world and get everything you've ever wanted, or it can be an emotionally toxic nightmare where you withhold your feelings, get all twisted up and angsty, blame others for your own emotional irresponsibility, and then go on wondering why your life is shit. At the moment, you're still comfortable with the latter path, with being the withdrawn, closed-hearted, bitter, angsty guy who feels hard done by life. So, to answer your question: Fear and dishonesty run your life. That's what you need to give attention to."

This critique felt more or less like being slapped in the face totally out of the blue. I wasn't prepared for such a thorough roasting, and found myself hunching over from the shock and impact of it.

Kevin continued: "There's a repeating lesson showing up for you here again. It's not that your fear, anxiety or frustration are bad, it's what you habitually do with them. If you bury those feelings, they just stew and gather energy, and you go toxic. But if you choose to face them and share them, there's a possibility for softening and opening - there's a pathway to light."

"You've been seeing this play out in your love life. When you shared your feelings with Tara, things went to heaven. When you withheld them from Tanisha, things went to hell. You had that same choice with me over the past few weeks, and unfortunately, you chose hell. Our time together could have been life-changing, open, safe and sacred for you, but your hiding kept that from happening. And here's the big takeaway: You have this choice moving forward, in every moment of every day, for the rest of your life. To be authentic or withhold, to open your heart or close it off. You're currently choosing to let your fear run your life, but by now you should know better."

When Kevin had finished delivering this assessment, he shifted back to a more casual, conversational tone. He thanked me again for all the help, adding that I should never agree to help someone if it isn't actually my truth, and we parted ways as I nursed a fresh bruise to my tender ego.

Chapter Ten

After Kevin moved into his new place, the two of us went on another brief hiatus from speaking. This gave me plenty of space to reflect on the patterns and lessons of mine he had once again brought to the surface. I realized during this self-reflection that despite achieving some personal breakthroughs here and there, my general tendency while moving through life was still to keep a closed heart, to bottle up my feelings, fears, needs, and insecurities. When I slipped into those patterns I would become a brittle, angsty person at best, and bring out a full-fledged monster to protect myself at worst.

During this time, I was working sporadically as an extra on film sets. This wasn't the most meaningful work in the world (possibly some of the least meaningful work, now that I think about it), but it sometimes paid well, didn't involve a routine, and therefore gave me a high level of freedom to devote most of my time to the more important task of excavating myself.

While I was diving deeper than ever into my inner work, the reality of my financial insecurity was often looming in the back of my mind, causing ongoing, constant stress and anxiety. The lack of routine in my work gave me plenty of free time, but it also meant inconsistent pay checks and often just scraping by with barely enough money for rent and the barest necessities.

Perhaps as a result of this ongoing financial insecurity, a particular scene from my childhood kept on coming up during my meditation sessions at this time. I would generally be sitting or laying down with my eyes closed, simply letting whatever feelings were present in me rise up to be felt, when this occurred.

The scene that kept resurfacing at these times took place when I was about five years old. My family had gone on a weekend trip to the city, and we were staying at my aunt and uncle's fancy, big new house. This trip was very exciting for me, and I had brought a little wallet which held all of the money I'd saved up to that point in my short life. My plan was to spend my savings on cool things at the malls and stores of the city. I don't remember exactly how much money was in that wallet of mine, but I think it was about fifty dollars. That was a significant fortune to me as a five-year-old. It was money I'd saved from little gifts of five or ten dollars that my grandparents had given me, and whatever small allowance I received for doing chores around the house. Altogether this had accumulated to a great savings that I was very proud of.

On the second day of our stay at my aunt and uncle's big fancy house, my wallet went missing. I couldn't find it in my little suitcase. I couldn't find it in the room I was staying in with my brothers. It was simply gone. After asking everyone if they had seen it and obsessively searching for it everywhere in the house, my little heart sank, and I realized my money was simply lost. When I told my parents about this, they seemed too preoccupied with other things to offer much consolation or reassurance. They told me I should be more careful with valuable things next time, and that was that.

As this memory resurfaced, I could feel the total devastation and heartbreak of my five-year-old self. He was still fully immersed in the confusion and sadness of that experience, feeling a sense of profound disappointment in life. He'd learned something very confusing during this experience: Money can be torn away from you at any moment. It's very unstable and scary. I couldn't help but wonder if my aversion to money as an adult - having spent many years living in the woods, more or less disconnected from the world of commerce - could in some small way be related to this early, formative experience.

There was a lot to ponder about this episode which kept coming up vividly during my meditations. One day when it resurfaced again, I had the sudden realization that my contemplation alone was a grossly insufficient response to it.

This occurred when I sat down to meditate one morning and once again the sad, dejected, five-year-old version of myself came into my awareness. Once again he felt crushed by the unfairness of life - that he could save all this money and have it disappear in an instant, and without anyone else caring. As I sat with, felt and witnessed this young part of me, I realized what a fool I'd been. He was showing up repeatedly, continuing to feel sad and frustrated, because nobody had ever done anything to correct what had happened all those years ago. His parents had failed him miserably, not seeing, understanding or validating him in any meaningful way. He'd been waiting decades for a person to come along and offer some kind of help, understanding, or support. He'd been waiting for someone to provide the kind of nurturance that he never experienced all those years ago. All he had experienced back then was a confusing loss and defeat. As I lay there with his hurt and frustration, I realized I was fully capable of helping him. I actually might have been the only person capable of helping.

There was an impatience and anger in me as this all became clear - I was angry that I hadn't stepped in to take care of him sooner, that up until this point I had simply been observing his pain, seemingly waiting for some benevolent person to show up one day and make things feel better. With a sense of urgency, I jumped up to my feet, put on a sweater, and seeing a clear vision of what would soothe this aching part of me, headed for the mall.

I didn't exactly stop the meditation I was in - I actually kept that child fully in my awareness as I hopped on my bike and rode to the nearest mall (which was exactly where he wanted to go). I asked him which store he would like to visit, so that we could look for a new wallet to replace the one that had been lost, and that's where we went. Then, as I looked at various wallets in that store, I asked him which one he thought was the coolest. Which one did he love?

He eventually chose a small, sleek wallet that felt cool and trendy to him. I bought it, and proceeded to throw out the ratty, old wallet I'd used for as long as I could remember. I had never actually liked this old wallet, but didn't ever think to replace it. After swapping it for my new, cool, inner child approved wallet, I went straight to the nearest ATM, where I got fifty dollars. I ceremoniously put this cash into the new wallet, finally replacing the lost savings from all those years ago. The lost wallet and lost fortune that my five-year-old self had been so flattened by were finally restored. He was extremely happy about this, and asked if he could spend all of the money in the wallet on candy. I told him he could spend it on whatever he wanted, candy included, but I wouldn't be eating any of it (I was abstaining from sugar at the time).

This experience was part of a very significant development for me. Suddenly, I had a firm sense of my inner child as something that was not a mere concept, but a very tangible aspect of myself that could be felt and spoken to. There was a very tender, vulnerable, authentic and unconditioned part of myself that I'd disowned, and that I was now coming back into relationship with. Sometimes it would surface in the form of myself at a specific stage of childhood, while at other times it would feel more broadly like my pure vulnerability or innocence. Feeling and connecting to this part of me seemed like one of the most enriching, beautiful, and sacred things possible.

When I shared this experience with Kevin, he quietly sent me fifty dollars electronically, along with the message: "This money is strictly for candy - that kid has good taste." He felt that this was a significant step forward in my journey (and was a candy lover himself).

"That is beautiful Miles," he shared. "I mean, you went out and did the very thing that your inner child should have experienced originally. What happened to you as a five-year-old, the way your parents completely failed to support or take care of this part of you, it's honestly disgusting. I can't even understand it, it's so grossly negligent to not see that this situation was a devastating emotional emergency that could so easily be healed with some love and support. It's unbelievable that you didn't get that - it seriously sickens me."

Kevin said these words with such conviction and anger - passionately validating and protecting the tender part of me that had felt so unseen and insignificant all those years ago, that I burst into tears.

"But what you just did," he continued, "is incredibly profound. You gave this broken and defeated part of yourself an experience that restored its sense of trust in life. It's literally perfection."

After this wallet experience, I began to initiate a variety of similar processes with my inner child regularly. Every day I would go inward, revisiting an assortment of barely remembered (by my conscious mind), emotionally charged incidents, with the intent of creating a corrective experience (that is, doing something life-affirming which hadn't been done at the time to protect my heart and my vulnerability). I went to scenes of schoolyard bullying and rewrote them, looking for a path that didn't involve shutting down, freezing, and being totally overwhelmed or dominated by the violence and energy of others. I went to scenes of early humiliation among peers, friends or family, and showed the young Miles - who was overwhelmed by shame and embarrassment - a bigger picture of what was happening. I showed him the insecurity, pain, and silliness behind the insults or judgements he felt crushed by, and I showed him the truth of his beauty, strength, and dignity. I helped him release the trapped energy and emotion he was holding. This became a daily practice, and a very joyful one. I almost always left these sessions with a big smile and tears across my face.

Something else happened in the wake of my wallet experience, which I'll share here just for the sake of curiosity and fun: My money problems rapidly transformed almost immediately following it.

This change began one day shortly after the wallet process, when I decided to try a manifestation technique I'd read about in a self-help book. The technique involved holding my hands over a glass of water, and imagining the energy of whatever it was that I wanted to manifest into my life flowing out of my hands and into the water. Since I was in need of money, I chose to focus on that. As I held my hands over a glass of water, I felt the energy of money flow out of them and infuse into the water. I visualized bills of currency suffusing into the liquid. Then I ceremoniously drank it and carried on with my day, completely forgetting about the little ritual shortly thereafter.

Over the course of that afternoon I got into quite a funk emotionally, and decided to go down to the river for a swim and to process some of the negativity that was swirling in me.

That turned out to be wise, as after a short swim, followed by venting my frustration and having a dialogue with it, I felt calm and confident that I would be able to take care of everything I'd been stressing about.

I lived at the top of a very steep hill at the time, and while I was biking up it on my way home from the river, I spotted a twenty-dollar bill on the curb. I stopped to pick it up, and then saw another bill a few feet ahead. Then I saw another, and another, and another. I got off my bike and walked up the hill collecting a wad of cash, as well as a couple of gift cards, which altogether totalled a value of maybe two or three hundred dollars. Even better than the money, however, was the joyful act of gathering it scattered on the ground like ripe apples strewn beneath an apple tree. It wasn't until later that night that I remembered the water exercise I'd done earlier in the day, and wondered if the two things were related.

A couple of days later, I got a very lucrative gig working as an extra on a high budget television show, making more per day than my month's rent. Kevin felt that this turn of events was connected to me restoring a basic trust in money, and life in general, to a very deep part of myself. This part of me had been carrying a sense of deflation and depression around money for decades, but after having a loving, supportive experience, it was no longer so closed to receiving it. My energy had shifted, and now my life was shifting, too. This period of unusual financial grace lasted for the following couple of months, and was a welcome reprieve from what I had been experiencing previously.

One day I asked Kevin if he was always connected to and in contact with his inner child - if that innocent, young, vulnerable part of him was constantly present in his awareness.

"Miles," he replied, "that part of me is *everything*. His voice is absolutely vital and necessary. He is totally honest, pure, unfiltered and natural. He's the most important part of me, and the only reason I can do anything that I do. I've learned how to have boundaries in order to take care of him, and I've learned to heal his hurt and confusion the way you are learning to do with yourself right now. But his purity? His honesty and perceptiveness? The grace underneath whatever pain he holds? I would be lost and hopeless without that. I don't get to make any decisions without his input. To ignore him would be inner child neglect. To act against his needs would be inner child abuse. And failing to understand and see clearly when he's triggered or coming from a wounded place would be negligent, too."

As I was going deeper into my inner work at this time, I began attempting to bring a new awareness into my daily life in different ways. One of the main ways I did this was my ongoing practice of going for walks in parks, along busy streets, or anywhere really, and consciously studying the emotional armouring I would normally automatically clad myself with. My intention was to remove it, or keep it from going up in the first place.

For nearly as long as I could remember, crossing paths with someone in a school hallway, on a sidewalk, or along any other pedestrian thoroughfare was often an experience in some combination of shame, avoidance, insecurity or inflated ego. As another individual approached me, I would often look in the opposite direction or to the ground and close myself off, falling into an automatic insecurity response. Physiologically, this felt like subtly constricting my whole body, becoming tense and unnatural. Emotionally, it felt like shutting off from my vulnerability, openness and joie de vivre by going into a safe, protective shell that seemed to compress all those more expansive, natural feelings. Often the more curious or drawn to someone I was, the more my armour would come out and engage, tightening me up, putting a wall between my heart and whoever I was crossing paths with. I'd gotten so used to this over so many years that I didn't fully realize what was happening until Kevin helped me understand what a closed heart felt like, and I developed a sense of what being open, natural, and free from shame felt like.

As a regular practice, I would go for a walk, and whenever someone approached me from the opposite direction, feel my insecurity begin to engage. I felt the part of me used to putting up a wall or putting on a mask rushing into action, and took a deep breath, intentionally pausing myself. I told this protective, insecure part of me that we were going to take down our wall, that we were removing our mask, because we were exploring a new way of taking care of ourselves. We could handle anything that might happen with our wall down, and if it was necessary at any moment we could put it back up. But the wall was keeping love and connection from penetrating into our life. It was doing more harm than good. The sense of safety and belonging it was trying to protect or provide, could only actually be experienced by going beyond it. We would have to risk exposing ourselves if we ever wanted to feel acceptance. We'd have to step out of our armour if we wanted to feel the tenderness of connection.

When I noticed my old protective pattern stirring on these walks, I would internally repeat to myself: "I'm taking the wall down now. I don't need it anymore. I'm taking my mask off now, it's time to be open." I would then try to really see whoever I was crossing paths with, without the barriers of shame, insecurity, comparison or self-consciousness clouding my perception. As I relaxed the tense parts of myself, sometimes with deep breaths, I tried to witness others through a lens of openness, curiosity, and sanctity, stepping into the belief (or truth) that everyone I crossed paths with was a divine soul and a potential beloved friend. Instantly, the results were astonishing.

Whenever I moved in the direction of this openness, the overwhelming majority of people I saw suddenly began smiling at me and offering warm greetings as I crossed paths with them. I wasn't initiating this, people just suddenly seemed to feel extremely comfortable with me. Sometimes I would cross paths with an individual who looked totally withdrawn and closed-hearted, with a big frown weighing down their face. But as I met eyes with them and maintained my open, heart-centred state, I watched their eyes light up and a deeply furrowed frown slowly break into a smile across their face. On one occasion I was watching a woman walk towards me in a city park, thinking to myself that everything happening in her life is part of some extraordinary masterpiece of learning and growth, including this moment. I was letting the beauty, profundity, and importance of her life sink in, and as she got near me, she spontaneously broke into a fit of laughter while staring warmly into my eyes.

Some people were naturally easier for me to maintain an open heart with, the elderly and young children falling firmly into this category. The most difficult group for me to open my heart with was, perhaps predictably, adult men. It only got more difficult the more similarities such men had with me. There was an absurdity and irony to this (considering this was the group of people I had the most in common with and could relate to the most deeply), but I felt my heart reflexively close and a sense of insecurity and competitiveness surface around a large majority of the men I crossed paths with. Often this felt like it was part of some primal, instinctive pissing contest that some men habitually engage in, where we see one another as mere competition in a brutish, constant struggle for power and attention (one group that was a notable exception to this dynamic was gay men - many of whom seemed to be blessedly free from this game, and had hearts that were beautifully open to other men). It required some experimentation and emotional gymnastics for me to find a way of relaxing my insecurity and competitiveness in this department.

One of my first signs of progress in navigating this dynamic occurred when I was out for a walk, and an attractive young heterosexual couple approached me. I immediately felt my ego begin to fixate on the female partner, wanting to attract her attention and flex itself in front of her to receive some kind of energy or validation, with no care whatsoever for the feelings and humanity of the man by her side.

I asked the insecure part of me that was present to imagine that this man actually really liked me, to imagine that this man and I were going to be very close friends in the future, and that he will care about me very much. My insecurity immediately relaxed, and I was able to feel calm and natural around the man and woman. I actually felt really open to them, and happy that they were getting to experience companionship and love together. Apparently my insecurity was pretty easy to win over in this situation, all it seemingly wanted was to feel a simple sense of being accepted or liked, and the mere act of imagining that was enough to open it up. And oftentimes, by opening my heart to someone in this way, they would feel comfortable opening up theirs in return, making what had been imagined real.

I experimented with these types of little shifts in perception regularly, most often attempting to stretch my imagination into seeing whatever person I was interacting or crossing paths with as a soul that had been born into an incredibly unique circumstance, and had experienced all sorts of unbelievable love, loss, betrayal, yearning, heartbreak, and joy as part of their sacred journey. This often moved me from closed-hearted bitterness to having eyes filled with tears at the beauty before me.

Another group that was somewhat difficult for me to maintain an open heart around, though in a very different way from adult men, was adult women, especially those I found attractive. Part of this was my insecurity and confusion about how to hold myself naturally and cleanly when any level of sexual attraction was present (or even might potentially be). As I began to recognize the ways I became frozen and twisted up in these situations, I began attempting to stay totally present to my body and my energy when feelings of attraction arose. When interacting with or even simply crossing paths with a woman I found attractive, I would breathe deeply, getting centred in a sense of inner stability and calmness, and try to stay grounded in my body, rather than disassociate because I was uncomfortable with what I was feeling. When I did twist up and feel anxious, I would own everything I was experiencing, look at it lightly, with a sense of humour and acceptance, then gently guide myself back into a relaxed state of openness. Maintaining this level of presence helped extract me from my insecurities and projections, and made it possible for me to be in the moment in a cleaner, more direct way. Most importantly, it made it possible for my heart to stay open.

Sometimes, when I saw a woman I was extremely attracted to, it felt as though my heart impulsively leapt out of my chest and toward her. There was an intensity to this that felt exhilarating, but I realized that what was really happening was my sense of power was jumping out of me and relocating to someone else. Whenever this happened, I felt quite weak and needy, as though the beautiful person I was fixated on held something I was desperately lacking. Needless to say, this got in the way of me being centred and stable in my open heart. It actually totally disconnected me from it.

There were many things I would do to navigate this feeling when it came up. One of them was to remind the insatiable, needy part of me that it didn't have to grasp or manipulate for love, ever. In fact, doing that pushes love away, because it disconnects us from our heart, which is the engine that builds it and the magnet that attracts it. Love is a bottomless, endless, infinitely available resource that can never be taken away or missed out on.

I would get the needy part of me to imagine that the beautiful woman he was fixated on wasn't a reminder of his emotional poverty and incurable sense of aloneness - they weren't showing him what he lacked, what he needed or what he desperately yearned for. They were showing him a kind of beauty that he gets to experience, either within himself or with another, at any moment. I would actively shower him with that experience myself, filling up the places where he felt empty with love, nurturance, a sense of belonging - whatever was at the core of his yearning in that moment.

During this period, there was a mantra I would repeat to myself often. It involved releasing the desire or need to be the smartest, most attractive, or in any other way superior individual at any moment in any situation. An insecure part of me often felt a pressure to perform or outshine others in some way, and understanding the deeper reasons for and implications of this compulsion helped me begin disassembling it. There was something incredibly powerful about holding the reality that people can like me exactly as I am. That by relaxing any need to be better, I'm making it possible to just be natural, to let go of all posturing, and truly connect with others. Whenever I held this intention in a social situation, it was like a weight was lifted from my shoulders as I relaxed into the comfort of just being real, being okay with all that I am, and all that I am not. I have no doubt that it made me a much more enjoyable person to be around.

In general, the more I practiced this heart opening, the more individuals lit up and responded to my presence. The likelihood of individuals saying hello, approaching me, or initiating a conversation with me skyrocketed - I suddenly felt that people really liked me, probably because they felt that I liked them and were responding in kind. I realized that when I could step beyond my insecurities, it seemed as though my heart *did* like everyone, and in a very pure, innocent way just wanted to be friends with everybody. When I was free from the need to appear smart, cool, superior or sexy, it felt like most of what remained was a very simple tenderness and love.

During this time I bumped into someone I went to high school with, and they shared how they'd always wanted to get to know me and be my friend when we were teenagers, but felt that I was too scary to talk to, describing me as "completely unapproachable." Many others had made similar comments and observations about me being intimidating or scary over the years. Sometimes my mere presence could make a room fall silent or make a person visibly tense up. It was incredible to witness this dynamic turn on its head completely when I chose to put down my armour and step beyond my insecurity. The truth of me - my deepest, most authentic self - was as mushy and sensitive as it gets. He just wanted to love people and be friends with everyone. Putting on a shield had been a way to protect that raw vulnerability from a world filled with wounded, sometimes unkind people. Taking that armour off was a way of actively forging a conscious path towards the kind of life my heart really wanted. There were still hurt people who could (and would) be closed off, harsh and mean in the world, but I now understood the depths and nuances of that, because I'd walked in their shoes. I knew the story of unprocessed pain, insecurity, and protective posturing inside out, so had a context to put that type of behaviour into. I knew that sometimes when you really just want to feel safe and loved, but don't know how to go about that, it can feel to others like you absolutely hate them.

One day I was out for a walk with a friend and suggested that we try something together: We would imagine that everyone we crossed paths with really liked us. Just as we were beginning this a couple of teenage boys approached us on skateboards, and I gazed at them with a wide-open heart, imagining they were good friends who really liked me. They spontaneously stopped, getting off their skateboards to say hello and ask us what we were up to for the night, as though we were potential friends who might have the word on a good party happening in the neighbourhood. We chatted briefly, and they warmly wished us a good evening. As we continued along, imagining everyone was excited to see us, we had a similar, magnetic effect on others we crossed paths with. The number of warm greetings, wide grins, and people interested in us for no particular reason was absurd, and we eventually broke into fits of laughter, almost rolling on the ground it was so unusual and comical what was happening. The behavioural response we were evoking seemed inexplicable and completely out of the ordinary. We were in a city that was notorious for being socially isolating, cold and unkind, yet suddenly it was as though we had flipped a switch and were in an almost surreal fantasy of friendliness.

In the mornings and evenings during this time, I was regularly practicing a meditation where I would simply focus on breathing into my heart. I suppose because one's breath goes into the chest, it's quite easy to focus on the physiological sensation of directing the breath into the heart. Sometimes noteworthy thoughts or feelings would surface during these meditation sessions, and I'd feel drawn to go into some kind of process with them. For the most part, however, I just breathed in and out of my heart, and experienced a glowing, warm sensation that would slowly build throughout the meditation. Some days the glowing was so intense I would be squirming and moaning as an almost unbearable feeling of light and warmth built in my chest.

Kevin thought this was a great practice, and called it massaging my heart open. I began to do this when I was on the bus, watching my fellow passengers and learning to cultivate or maintain a feeling of radiant heart energy when a smelly, loud-breathing man sat down beside me and proceeded to eat potato chips with an open mouth. I'd do it during interactions with friends and acquaintances and feel myself loosen up and become more present.

One time, when I asked Kevin what he felt would be the best way to help open my heart, he told me to try and see my life the way my soul does. "Imagine you've lived a thousand lifetimes, Miles. Imagine the sense of maturity, grace, and dignity that would come with that. How much less anxious would you be to fulfill your fleeting, egoic desires? How quick would you be to judge and cut others out of your heart if you'd already stooped to their most shameful lows and done much worse across your vast reservoir of experience? How devastated and ungrounded would you be by the fleeting slights, rejections and losses of this life when you could really see the bigger picture and hold it for the hurt and fearful parts of yourself? How different would the closed hearts of those you encounter in the world feel if you maintained an awareness of the context within which such a phenomenon forms? How would your whole life, and everything you experience day to day look if you held this expansive vantage point for yourself? One thing is certain: Your heart would be more open more of the time."

I would attempt to stretch into this big picture perspective when I was confronted by individuals who were extremely closed, harsh or mean. I attempted to see the totality of the individual before me, imagining what devastation might have hurt them and injured their heart, and I would try to see the purity burning beneath whatever walls they'd erected to protect that pain. Sometimes I'd be bored waiting for a bus and begin doing this with a stranger, then find myself crying within seconds of really looking at them through this lens. I found myself crying more and more often, and confronting some of my shame around that. Given that it now seemed necessary for me to welcome my tears, not suppress them, even when they began flowing at random in public places, I had to challenge the parts of myself that still felt controlled by a collective stigma around crying. As I let myself cry in public more, the main thing I noticed was that people generally just avoid the crying guy. They'll usually turn the other way, either embarrassed for me or uncomfortable with the display of emotion, giving me the space to do my own thing.

Around this time, I decided to get a job as a server in a restaurant. Although not a glorious line of work by any means, a part of me had always thought that it would be a fun and interesting experience to interact with people in that particular role. Given that I'd spent so many years removed from society living in the woods, there was a certain novelty in it for me. There was also something appealing about having a job that involved receiving tips, because unlike a fixed hourly wage, tips would theoretically reflect my energy in each moment. In the same way that Kevin would go to the casino when he felt his energy was soaring and win a pile of money in twenty minutes, I expected the tips I received to be a direct representation of where I was at internally. As I got into the rhythm of a new job waiting tables, that indeed seemed to be the case.

After learning the basics of the position (memorizing the restaurant's menu, becoming adept at moving rapidly and multitasking), managing my energy and emotion was the most significant factor that would determine what kind of money I earned from night to night.

For example, if I had slipped into a depressive funk or a state of frustration and angst before a shift, my experience at work would always seem to reflect that internal conflict in clear ways. I might serve tables that were condescending and rude, that tipped nothing, or I may suffer from any variety of miscommunications and mistakes throughout the evening.

A habitual response to these unpleasant experiences would be to get even more upset, frustrated, and closed-hearted. Knowing this wasn't a fruitful path to take, I instead developed a habit of quickly going to a quiet corner of the restaurant or the staff washroom and doing some emergency emotional processing whenever I noticed my heart was severely shut down and I was filled with toxic energy. I would attempt to shift whatever anger, frustration or disappointment was flooding my system and closing my heart, in serious instances maybe venting some rage at the bathroom mirror, then returning to work after having taken an emotional dump.

When I was able to maintain an open heart - to really be gracious, unselfconscious and naturally caring toward those I served with no expectation of reward or desire for reciprocation, I was often tipped very generously. And even when I wasn't, my open heart meant that it actually didn't matter - I was already experiencing and rooted in something infinitely more valuable than a bit of paper money.

The number of times I caught myself getting deeply sad or angry because someone was rude or didn't tip was embarrassing, but it was also a great opportunity for growth. Every time this happened, I told myself: "Miles, if you are this emotionally affected over a few dollars or a stranger's attitude, you've got issues," and then tried to hold a bigger, more gracious and relaxed perspective, where such petty grievances were obsolete.

Over time I found it easier to go into that open-hearted, bigger picture perspective day in day out, and really enjoyed getting to meet and interact with what was essentially a river of humanity that moved through the restaurant. I played little energetic games where I would look at a table I was about to serve from afar before greeting them, and mentally or emotionally establish a loving connection with them before saying hello. I would form a deep sense of reverence and respect for their souls, and then begin my interaction with them from there.

One of the greatest gifts of this job was getting to be around all of my coworkers over a period of time. I got to bear witness to my insecurity and closed heart as I began working in a new environment with new people, and then walk myself into opening up, being more natural, and challenging my tendency to hide behind a wall. Learning how to be comfortable and authentic around my coworkers was an amazing challenge and gift. As someone who considered himself a lifelong outsider, it was easy for me to feel somewhat alien around everyone I worked with. There were many seemingly normal things I simply couldn't relate to as someone who had lived a rather unusual life (I didn't drink alcohol, party, or have any interest in sports, film, television, cars, etc). I realized my feeling of 'otherness' wasn't fully rooted in truth, however. Every one of my coworkers had an evolving heart, had experienced loss, love, betrayal, joy, inspiration, insecurity, hope, shame and defeat. In this sense, at a fundamental level everyone was totally relatable, I just needed to stop believing the absurd story that I was wildly weird or unique, and engage with their common humanity.

I noticed that opening up my heart was much easier with some of my coworkers than others. As you'd expect, the people who were more open and kind themselves, were generally easier to be open around. Whenever I found my heart habitually clenching up around a specific coworker - usually someone who seemed cold, detached and unkind towards me - I made it my homework to study why I was reacting by closing myself off, and to look into who they really were. I would sometimes do this by asking them questions about their life, to try and better understand the emotional dynamics at play in them, and often this would result in my softening. Often once I realized what I was doing, I'd just stop closing off around them. I'd greet them with openness, refuse to take their closedness personally or react by closing myself, and make a point of being warm to them regardless of how they responded to me. In some cases, I had the pleasure of watching as they slowly softened and warmed to my presence.

Although this job didn't exactly feel like my life's purpose, it was a lot of fun, and the fact that I was rewarded nightly for managing my emotions, connecting to my heart and being kind to others gave it a deeper meaning.

I'd been at my job as a server for a few months when Kevin called me up one day and said that he felt it was time for me to write a book. "You've done your work," he declared. "I've been looking at things for a while now, and it's very clear that you are ready to write a book. You can hold something very pure and authentic now, and it's the only thing that makes sense for you to be doing."

Chapter Ten

I had mixed feelings about Kevin's new perspective. At this point in time I'd more or less let go of my dreams of writing some profound work of beauty and wisdom. I wasn't sure I wanted to jump back into that or build up any hope in myself, regardless of Kevin's thoughts on the matter.

One layer of my reluctance was likely related to the fact that for several years at this point, I had been actively dismantling my ego. As part of this process, I had deconstructed the solid sense of self that previously supported my identity as a confident person in the world. This teardown seemed necessary in order for me to really honestly look at myself in a deeper, more humble way, but it also meant that I was no longer very confident at all. I actually had become quite collapsed in my sense of confidence. Kevin saw this clearly, observing that I needed to rebuild a healthy ego (a healthy sense of self) after tearing it down for so long.

"It's not about completely eradicating all ego, Miles," he said. "That's not healthy or even possible. You need some sense of self to simply move around in this world and maintain a basic level of psychological autonomy and coherence. The key is to have a balanced ego. You need a balanced, healthy sense of self and healthy boundaries. A healthy ego is mature and graceful. It isn't married to insecurity or wounds, and it doesn't need to act out to overcompensate for them. A healthy ego is rooted in a humble yet strong sense of self, comfortable with being wrong and imperfect because it is so firmly connected to its own inherent goodness."

The fact that I needed to rebuild a healthy sense of self sounded true, but jumping back into working on a book was something I had no interest in. After a few months of Kevin more or less insisting that I do so, however, my resistance eroded and I slowly, tentatively began playing around with some creative ideas.

"You have full permission to write anything we've spoken about," Kevin said. "Whatever you want to do, you have my blessing. There are certain things I think you'd be better suited to write about than others, but you should do whatever you feel drawn to."

I gradually began devoting time to regular brainstorming, writing and visioning, and slowly a potential book started to take shape. Over a few months, I was able to more or less write an entire first draft of that book, which discussed some of the things I'd been learning over the previous several years. That project was not the book you are currently reading, however. Some things happened that prevented me from ever finishing that book, and changed everything completely.

Chapter Eleven

For the entire time that I knew Kevin, he was sick. It was sometimes easy for me to forget that he had a chronic illness keeping him from fully living his life, as he managed to meet the world with so much resilience and strength. But behind his larger than life persona and irrepressible passion, a cloud of pain and frustration hovered around Kevin constantly.

He would often spend days in bed, his head burning in pain, suffering a kind of brain fog that he described as nightmarish and torturous. I suspect that his hypersensitivity to the energy of others and heightened intuition only made this experience more difficult and disorienting. Many days he would call me simply to talk to someone with a calm, stable nervous system, using me as a kind of anchor to help relax and ground his frazzled mind and body.

There were lots of ups and downs with Kevin's illness over the years, but during the fall after he moved to Vancouver, he reached a more challenging place than I'd ever previously witnessed. Part of this was related to his growing frustration with the limitations of his life. Kevin was an extremely gifted person, and he knew it. The number of stories he had demonstrating his intuitive brilliance were vast. These abilities, combined with his deep, penetrating understanding of people's vulnerability and tenderness, made him someone I considered a true genius. And yet his life was quite small, so to speak. Sometimes I alone made up his entire circle of friendship and support. Despite his brilliance, he was not a well-known teacher touching the hearts of countless people across the world. On the contrary, he lived a tenuous life where some days it was a struggle just to get out of bed or pay the rent. He felt that his wings were clipped by his illness, and though his willingness to explore pathways to healing was remarkably strong, over time I watched his fatigue and cynicism grow.

During this fall when things began to get particularly bleak, a couple of situations brought additional stress into Kevin's life. The first of these was a messy, acrimonious breakup he went through with a woman he'd been in a relationship with over the previous year.

After sharing a very deep, close, loving connection, he and his girlfriend decided it would be best to take a break so that she could focus on herself without Kevin's often overwhelming influence. Having a larger than life, hyper-intuitive presence like Kevin in one's world could often make a person feel as though they didn't have a firm grasp on their own internal compass and an autonomous sense of self. His strong perceptions and insights could interfere with an individual's process of listening to their own voice, causing them to feel disempowered and weak.

As I understood it, he and his girlfriend ended things in a mutual way, on very good terms, and continued visiting one another almost daily. Conflict arose when his now ex-girlfriend suddenly began seeing another man and didn't tell Kevin. As Kevin explained it, he and his ex were still occasionally sleeping together, so when he found out about her new partner more or less by accident, he was shocked and deeply hurt. A vulnerable part of him felt betrayed and dishonoured by someone he had deeply trusted.

Despite his wisdom and awareness, Kevin was still a very vulnerable, and in some ways fragile man. Issues around fidelity and trust touched very deep, raw places in him. Because of this, I completely understood why he was hurt by the way things had played out with his ex in this situation. She didn't seem to have been intentionally hurtful, but by failing to communicate everything going on clearly and honestly with Kevin, there was a breach of trust, and a part of him hadn't been taken care of or respected. Because this woman was someone he'd opened up to very deeply, and they were still being intimate together here and there, her lack of communication felt confusing and painful.

I believe that the two of them got into some kind of argument about this situation before cutting off all communication with one another, with mutual feelings of resentment and anger, and no sense of resolution.

Kevin's deep tenderness and vulnerability were qualities I loved and respected about him. I'd never known a man to be so aware of his insecurities, capable of owning up to them, and not feel that it was unacceptable to be in process with them. I'd read authors and heard teachers talk about vulnerability with the emotional distance and safety of an academic or master, but Kevin actually showed a living, conscious vulnerability to me in the flesh. He was never shy to own his deep, lingering insecurities, inhabiting the extraordinarily sensitive heart that was also capable of such profound understanding, perception and grace.

Knowing Kevin's history and his wounds, the fact that he was extremely hurt by the way this breakup played out was not surprising. The depth to which it affected him and the way his pain around it lingered, however, was somewhat of a shock.

He quickly began seeing another woman after this breakup, entering into a connection that was short-lived. Soon after that ended, he saw another woman briefly, and as soon as that ended, he was dating again. I knew Kevin could process things and metabolize emotions very rapidly, but I could feel that this wasn't what was happening here. He was on a rebound, moving towards distractions rather than sitting with and fully moving through the pain and sadness left in the wake of what he'd just gone through.

During this time, Kevin had also stepped up the alternative healing therapies that he was employing to combat his Lyme disease (he had previously tried a variety of more conventional treatments to no avail). The most extreme of these protocols was something called bee venom therapy, which involved stinging oneself with numerous live bees regularly.

I won't pretend to know what this stinging therapy is supposed to do biologically, but according to Kevin, many people had anecdotal reports of fully healing themselves from chronic Lyme disease by practicing this rather masochistic protocol.

Over the course of several months, Kevin kept a small colony of bees, first in his apartment, then on the roof of his building, and methodically stung himself many times every other day or so. This involved picking up a live bee with a pair of tweezers and pressing it against a specific area on his back. I think he told me about stinging himself this way up to fourteen times in one session. Needless to say, Kevin was committed to healing, by whatever means necessary.

The symptoms of his illness, however, were getting progressively worse regardless of his ongoing efforts (or maybe because of them). He occasionally alluded to giving up altogether sometime in the near future if nothing came of the great effort he was putting into healing, though I wasn't entirely sure what that meant.

Chapter Eleven

Throughout this autumn, my conversations with Kevin seemed to get progressively more bleak. He was not in a good place emotionally in the wake of his breakup, he was in a precarious place financially, and his illness was worsening. At the end of November, I lent him some money to help cover rent and basic expenses while he was in a tight spot, and felt certain that things would return to normal for him soon enough. They always had in the past.

My life at this time, in contrast, was feeling unusually good. I quit my job as a waiter to work on writing a book full time, and was feeling more connected to people and the world than I had in ages. After years of living a more or less monastic, solitary life, I was beginning to meet some new people and engage with the world more actively. I had moved into a downtown apartment near the ocean, and felt more optimistic about life than ever.

Slowly, however, Kevin's challenges began to consume more of my attention and energy. Almost immediately after leaving my job, I ended up lending Kevin some more money, which felt like an obvious thing to do for a friend in need, but put a significant dent in the modest savings I'd planned on living off while writing.

Kevin was no stranger to financial ups and downs. He earned his livelihood as an empathic facilitator, and he was truly remarkable at what he did. But because of his personal disposition, he didn't ever engage in any active marketing or promotion of his work whatsoever. Even his simple website looked incredibly outdated, like it could have been designed ten or fifteen years earlier. Kevin seemed to like it that way - it meant that no one was drawn to him because of sleek marketing, a captivating image or superficial fluff. All of his work came to him through word of mouth. Because he was so talented, there was generally a steady stream of enthusiastic clients for his work, but during this period that had vanished.

Rather than drum up some sort of marketing campaign, however, Kevin's approach was to resolve whatever was causing his lack of work by addressing what was going on with him emotionally and energetically. I'd seen this strategy work for him many times in the past, though something about this particular situation seemed different.

Our conversations at the time generally consisted of Kevin doing a variety of emotional work on himself from different angles. It was a bizarre thing to observe that my teacher was the one whose wounds seemed most difficult to heal, but that's often how it appeared as I watched and listened to him explore all sorts of deep recesses within himself. In contrast, I seemed incredibly simple to work on emotionally. Cracking through my protective shell of insecurity, anger or resistance and into the mushy tears and tenderness that lie underneath wasn't very difficult or complex, it was actually pretty straightforward. My heart seemed easy to nudge open. Kevin, however, seemed to contain depths that were more difficult to reach, or more clever and stubborn in their resistance to change.

On more than one occasion during this period, Kevin talked about the possibility of ending his life. This was actually something I'd heard Kevin speak about since I first met him eight years earlier. It was always brought up as a thought mentioned in passing, something Kevin confessed to considering as a last resort if his health didn't ever improve. When that thought resurfaced during this period, I tried to be understanding of what Kevin was going through, and told him that I was there to support him in figuring out how to keep on living. I knew he wasn't bringing the subject up to get attention or as an emotional outburst - he was bringing it up as a sick person who wondered if their best option moving forward was to leave their aching body behind. If history was any indication, however, these thoughts and remarks wouldn't go anywhere. Kevin would, in all likelihood, have some emotional process that brought him back to his light, subsequently make a bunch of money, and carry on with life. That's what always happened.

For the time being, however, things continued to get only bleaker in his world, and I found myself being subsumed by that. I was so close to Kevin and so involved in his process that it seemed to blend with my own. The distinction between what he was going through and my own life as a separate individual was often blurred.

As this was happening, I began to develop some of the same strange neurological symptoms Kevin suffered from. I started to get a feeling of swelling in my head whenever I went on my computer or looked at the screen of my phone, one of the major symptoms Kevin suffered from with his illness. This was pretty worrying for me, and meant that I suddenly had to more or less avoid using any screened devices.

When I described these symptoms to Kevin, he said that they sounded exactly like his electromagnetic sensitivity. It seemed that I was not only taking on what he was going through emotionally, but I was also taking on his illness, and the prospect of that was somewhat terrifying.

One evening I sat down alone in my apartment and decided to look at all of the heavy emotions I was carrying as a result of Kevin's situation and my role within it. I closed my eyes, tuned into my feelings, and quickly tapped into a vein of strong anger. I began to scream and shout (living in an apartment with thin walls, I had learned the art of 'quiet screaming,' which is the practice of screaming at a very low volume, but with full emotional intensity). Pounding my fists and swearing, I raged and pushed the sense of being burdened and smothered by Kevin's energy, toxicity and heaviness out of my system. I passionately owned and gave a voice to all of the things that had felt bad about being around him, and let myself have a strong boundary with his energy. My anger acted like a fire burning everything that I'd taken on to ashes, restoring my boundaries and a distinct sense of self. It was a very intense, cathartic process, with a lot of growling, swearing and quiet screaming. When I felt that I had completed expressing these feelings, I went for a walk to the grocery store. As I moved along the sidewalk in the cool evening air, I felt like I had just aged in reverse ten or fifteen years. I felt light, buoyant, vibrant and free. I felt absolutely amazing, filled with a deep sense that life was fresh, hopeful and bright. I knew I had to tell Kevin.

When we spoke about this experience, I wondered aloud if it meant that I should take care of myself by stepping away from our connection for a while. That was basically what I'd done during my process - I'd pushed Kevin's reality out of me, and told the collapsed parts of myself that his energy was not their energy or their burden to carry, that it was someone else's and we could let it go.

Kevin felt that I was missing the bigger picture of what was happening.

"You have a lesson here that you aren't seeing clearly, Miles," he said. "What you did during that process was protect your inner child. You pushed some heavy, scary energy out of your system, and restored a safe space for him to breathe and relax in. Because he'd taken on my stuff and had become overwhelmed by it, this felt really good. You took care of your vulnerability and cleaned your energy out. Now, you can leave it at that and step away from this dark and scary situation, or you can help that vulnerable part of yourself grow by showing him how to be safe within the darkness. You can go feel happy and secure in the gentleness away from this drama, or you can choose to evolve, to learn how to hold light in the face of pain, hopelessness and confusion.

"I think this is a very big lesson. You've totally failed to hold light throughout this last chapter of our connection. You've let yourself believe and be convinced by my despair and frustration. You've let my consciousness dominate your own. I mean, that's why you've gotten my symptoms. You're not having proper boundaries, you're not staying connected to your truth and to your light in the face of my overwhelm. Your resolve in the face of pain and conflict are being tested, and you get a failing grade on that level so far, Miles. You haven't been holding truth for yourself, you haven't been processing your fear and overwhelm when they come up. You've let your emotions and my energy disconnect you from your heart and your sense of self.

"And to be clear, that's not what I want or need from you right now. I don't want someone to commiserate with me or to get meek and collapsed around all of my frustration and angst. I want you to hold light for me! I want you to tell me why I'm totally full of shit when I am stuck in my hopelessness and believing my cynicism. When I'm stuck in fear and negativity, I want you to contradict me and point out how I'm being negligent with the truth and talking from a totally wounded place. I want you to interrupt me when I'm stuck in a sense of distrust in life and tell me that I've lost the plot. That's what I need right now, and you've failed me. You've failed yourself, too. And you get to walk away, no one is forcing you to stay with this situation right now. You will almost certainly feel better in the short term if you pull back from me. But you won't grow. You can't really hold light for others in this world if you are afraid of and overwhelmed by their pain and darkness, if their wounds scare you and disconnect you from your heart."

Kevin was saying probably the most profound thing I'd ever heard. It was true, I'd completely collapsed under the weight of his situation, and given the symptoms I was developing, walking away was tempting. But looking at the bigger picture he was presenting, that wasn't an option. I needed to learn how to take care of myself in the midst of all this drama, to hold light in the dark, and not simply run for the safety of my shell where there was no human complexity (or human connection) to hurt me (or enrich me).

After this conversation ended, I turned off the lights in my apartment, sat on my couch, and closed my eyes. I felt a part of myself that was completely terrified by this entire situation. This part of me felt like a sensitive child who just wanted peace and stability in his home. To him Kevin felt like an erratic, alcoholic uncle who would barge into his world at any given moment, bringing a storm of drama, trauma, confusion and pain. This part of me felt very much the way any child would feel about a scary grown-up who destabilized their world - he didn't like them and wanted them to go away. He reflexively cringed and closed down whenever that chaos arrived in his life, and at this point he felt like it was almost always present. Consequently, he was almost always in a defensive, fearful state.

I sat and observed what this part of me was feeling, trying to understand all he was going through and why he saw things the way he did, asking simple questions to help me see his perspective. I totally understood why he was so upset about Kevin's presence in his world, but I told him that there was a very specific reason why Kevin was coming around: He wasn't actually an aimless, lost soul coming to us with no purpose. Kevin was coming to us because he thought we might be able to help him. And Kevin was very much open to whatever help we might be able to offer. He was coming to us because we had something special that he thought could be beneficial to his life.

This part of me completely lit up at that idea. The notion that he could offer something to support a person in need transformed his energy from avoidance and overwhelm to excitement and enthusiasm. He suddenly felt a purpose in this situation.

I continued to explain that the way we could help Kevin the most was to maintain our sense of separateness, personal power and light around him. It was of the utmost importance for us to take care of ourselves, and make sure we felt as amazing as possible, so we could share some of our good feelings with Kevin and offer a different perspective, one that came from a place that was firmly rooted in our distinct sense of self.

The more I explained this context of our relationship with Kevin, the more my inner child became animated, energized and proud that he might have something special to offer a friend. It was quite a dramatic and rapid shift.

I was visualizing this entire conversation with my inner child, and in my visualization we were in a house together. I thought of this house as a container for our personal energy. In order to keep our personal energy strong and clear, I suggested that we build a special room in the house specifically for Kevin, so that whenever he visited us his energy and reality were kept separate from ours. I then created this new room, with a glass wall separating it from the main living space. This clear glass wall acted as a boundary that would allow us to see, interact with and help Kevin, but would keep his energy separate from ours.

After this room was finished, I suggested that my inner child fill the rest of the house with his energy, and cleanse out whatever heavy feelings had accumulated around the house with his own pure light. When this process felt complete, I opened my eyes and got ready for bed.

The next day when I spoke with Kevin, I prepared before our conversation by evoking all the same inner imagery I'd played with the previous night. I imagined the house, explained to my inner child that we were about to invite Kevin over and help him, then prepared Kevin's special room.

When I got onto the phone with Kevin, I imagined him going into that room, while my inner child and I stood on the other side of its glass wall with a clear purpose of helping our special friend to the best of our abilities.

Kevin wanted to process some particularly heavy emotions and wounds related to his childhood, which on a practical level meant exploring and giving a voice to some very deep, hurt and confused parts of himself. As he dove into this, I noticed my inner child getting a bit afraid of the intensity and harshness of the emotions Kevin was excavating, so I explained to him what was happening. I showed him that Kevin was cleaning himself emotionally, and visualized a shower head over Kevin bathing him in his special healing room while he continued to process difficult emotions. All of the intense feelings Kevin was giving a voice to were part of this cleaning, I explained. Once my inner child understood that this was the context of what was happening, he got very excited and began to cheer Kevin on. As Kevin continued to feel into and vocalize his intense feelings, my inner child and I repeated every word he uttered silently to ourselves, as though we were adding our support to everything he said.

Kevin continued processing for some time, at one point pausing to ask me what I was doing. He felt as though I was actually processing him, and it was having a very strong, positive effect on his energy. I explained to him what I'd been doing internally, and he felt that his suspicions were confirmed. "I could feel you lifting me and carrying me as I was processing," he explained, "it made what I was doing feel so much more powerful, having someone hold that support alongside me. Please keep on doing it!"

I began relying on this inner practice every time I spoke with Kevin. Given everything I'd witnessed and learned with him over the years, it was my best attempt at taking care of the frightened part of me by actively showing it the bigger picture of what was going on, and keeping it engaged in that awareness moment to moment. And it appeared to be working. Rather than feeling deflated and overwhelmed by our conversations, I began feeling charged up and enlivened by them. Rather than collapsing into passivity and silence during them, I would often offer contrary views and perspectives. When Kevin would give a voice to feelings of abject hopelessness, I would say how this was all simply a temporary experience, and was guaranteed to shift. "That's really true," Kevin would humbly respond.

In addition to practicing my active inner child-minding during our conversations, I also developed a pretty rigorous practice of emotional work during this period. Several times a day I would engage in some form of processing, setting a timer on my phone to ensure I devoted a certain period solely to feeling what was going on inside of me, letting it move, and holding truth for it.

Much to my relief, the symptoms I'd been developing (mostly a constant pressure in my head that was aggravated by computer or phone use) completely vanished after a few days of doing this emotional work. Kevin could feel the shift in my energy, and commented that whatever I was doing, I should keep on doing it. Kevin's situation hadn't changed, nor had my degree of involvement with it, but the way I was holding myself within it was completely different. It wasn't flattening me anymore. I was maintaining a sense of separateness that did not require closing my heart, and actually allowed me to be more present and caring. I was maintaining a level of autonomy, strength and balance that made it possible for me to be fully available to help my friend.

I wish I could say this was the end of the story, and that I indefinitely mastered some high emotional art and saved the day. But, as it unfolded, things were more complex. Kevin's condition continued to deteriorate, and I slipped from my place of balance and strength here and there. While the situation at hand was stretching me to grow, there were moments, hours and days where I dropped back into feeling overwhelmed and flattened by it.

One afternoon during this time, Kevin and I went for a walk together in Stanley Park, a large forested area near downtown Vancouver that I was lucky to live on the edge of. We spoke at length about various things he was exploring relative to his healing, and then turned our attention to the book that I'd been working on. Kevin had strongly encouraged me to write a book for about a year at this point, and I had more or less finished the first draft of a manuscript. With all that was happening, however, I'd put the book on hold, and we discussed how I might move forward with it.

Kevin looked into the energy of everything, and had some stark observations to share: "When I look at you putting a book into the world, I still see your ego getting extremely inflated and running amok from whatever amount of worldly success you experience. I see the wounded parts of you getting drunk off of the attention and acceptance from others, and how that can totally disconnect you from your heart."

As Kevin shared this, he went into what he called 'facilitator mode,' which meant we were no longer having a normal, person-to-person, conversation, but that he was now acting as an unfiltered mouthpiece for whatever energy he was feeling and seeing.

"Yes," he continued, "there's such a massive potential for your worst tendencies to be fed by becoming a successful author. I have no doubt that what you've written right now is brilliant and would profoundly help people. And I think you should still publish it, but you have to be incredibly humble with these wounded parts of yourself and keep your feet on the ground if you want to do it in a healthy way. Can you see what I'm saying?"

This was a difficult question to answer. All I knew was that because of my predisposition towards fear and closing my heart in the face of adversity, I'd recently developed a neurological condition. Given that, I could very easily eat humble pie, and agree that I still had some work to do.

Kevin continued: "Again, I think you should still publish whatever you've written, but you have to be very aware of the wounded parts of yourself getting high off of any amount of success. You have to be extremely conscious of what that does to your heart, how that might inflate you and make you delusional. You've come a long way, Miles, but these parts of you can still totally hijack your consciousness. What's been happening lately is a perfect example of that - you've dropped the ball and let your fear overwhelm you. Navigating success and keeping yourself grounded is going to require some real humility and discipline. If you let your ego get inflated chronically, it won't be pretty."

I quietly listened, taking in all that Kevin was saying.

"Everything depends on you coming back to your heart," he continued. "That's the key for everyth...."

Kevin stopped mid-sentence, bending down to pick something up off the ground of the dirt path we were walking along. When he stood up, he was holding a rust discoloured key that had been dropped on the trail in his open palm, staring into my eyes: "That's your *key* Miles! That's your key to everything! Humility, your heart, that's your key! Do you understand the significance of this?" Kevin handed me the key and continued: "You need to put this on a necklace or something and wear it. You can never, ever forget this. You're in process. You need to stay humble and remember what your key is for the rest of this lifetime. It's your heart."

I didn't put that key on a necklace, not yet at least, though I do still have it and treasure it.

A day or two after this conversation, Kevin and I had a chat on the phone to follow up on some of the things that had come up during it. We were speaking about the same stuff (my writing, and the hurt parts of me that craved attention in unhealthy ways) and Kevin reinforced the importance of keeping my ego in a state of balance and integrity.

During this conversation, Kevin said something that shocked me. He was talking passionately about my toxic ego, and about how men like me (with toxic egos) dominate the world, control everyone, and get everything they want in life, when something felt very off. I'd been getting to know what it sounded and felt like when my wounds were triggered and doing the talking, either in my head or in conversation with others, and what I was hearing Kevin say sure felt and sounded like it was coming from a wound.

I got Kevin to pause, and asked him if he believed what he was saying, or if he knew it was coming from a wounded part of him. He immediately recognized that it was indeed a wounded part of him talking. It was a young part that was triggered by male power, because of his upbringing and his childhood relationship with his father. I could certainly relate. At that moment, however, I was aware enough to see that Kevin was triggered, and that he was projecting onto me. I don't doubt that he was seeing and naming something real in me during our conversation - I did and do contain places within myself that are insecure and compensate for that by acting like a callous, alpha male. In that moment, however, Kevin's wounds were adding an emotional charge to what he was seeing that wasn't clean or grounded in reality. He wasn't having a naked experience of the present, his vision was distorted by the unresolved pain of the past. A part of him was freaking out and villainizing me, instead of seeing the bigger picture, which is that my obnoxious ego is not actually powerful at all, it's insecure. It is the very embodiment of weakness and disempowerment. It was and is the opposite of big and scary, it's a hurt boy. And it most definitely is not the force that rules this world - divinity (or truth, or love) does that.

This was a fascinating moment, because I could only see what I was seeing in Kevin thanks to the work I'd been doing on myself, work that was guided by him. And when I pointed out that it appeared as though he was triggered, he wasn't upset or embarrassed. He completely owned that he was indeed triggered and projecting onto me, and was excited to explore that. There was no facade of perfection that Kevin had to get defensive about if a vulnerability was exposed, he was as sincere in his commitment to truth as one could be.

Acknowledging that there was projection happening here led to a lengthy exploration, and the realization that this was by no means the first time such a dynamic had taken place between us. We spoke about Kevin's insecurities coming up in relation to me, and he owned that there was a very wounded part of him, a part that didn't trust confident or successful men, that sometimes felt threatened by me and distorted his perception.

"Oh this burns, Miles," he said, as he felt the discomfort of being completely honest with all that was present. "I'm so embarrassed - this part of me completely lacks integrity. It's so disconnected from truth! And it has been - I have been - totally out of line and unfair to you, in a subtle way, because of its insecurity. I'm truly sorry." Kevin paused to breathe for a few moments before continuing. "I'm so glad you brought this up. Please, please, always hold me accountable when you see these things. This burning is what I live for! I need to see these parts of myself and bring them into the light."

Kevin's sincerity and willingness to own all that was going on, however unpleasant it may have been, was amazing. Part of me felt quite uncomfortable thinking that Kevin's wounds had an impact on how he related to me, given the influence I'd allowed him to have in my life. Even if it was only very subtle, infrequent and outweighed by all the good of our connection, an innocent part of me had to really step back and process the fact that Kevin could sometimes be very triggered by me and see things unclearly. Like everyone else I'd ever met, he was complex, fallible and human. This was something I already knew, but another nuance to his complexity had revealed itself, and it took a while for me to wrap my head around it.

After having some time to reflect on all of this, I wondered if the fact that Kevin could be so triggered by my ego actually made him the perfect teacher. He was so hypersensitive to and repulsed by this part of my person that he brought it to the surface in a very loud, clear, unrelenting way for me to witness. It seemed kind of ideal.

This conversation felt like it marked a significant shift in my dynamic with Kevin. My inner work had made it possible for me to more clearly see and recognize when others were in their own wounds. Even with someone as persuasive and compelling as Kevin, I was developing the ability to sense when something was off emotionally or energetically, and name that. What this opened up was nothing short of amazing.

Kevin and I had been talking every day for months when he suddenly stopped answering my calls and texts. My initial thought was that he was taking yet another break from our connection, and maybe decided that this wasn't important enough to make a big announcement about.

After a few days without hearing from him, however, I got worried. I sent more texts, and still received no response. I reached out to a mutual friend who I knew had also been in contact with Kevin at the time. She hadn't heard from him either, and was experiencing the same anxiety about his well-being that I was.

When Kevin's landlord called me one afternoon to ask if I knew where he was, sharing that Kevin wasn't responding to calls or messages and hadn't been seen at his building since I'd last heard from him, it became clear that Kevin wasn't just keeping to himself, he was missing.

Being chronically sick and financially strapped, the idea that Kevin had gone on some kind of spontaneous trip without telling anyone seemed very unlikely and out of character. Over the eight years that I had known him, he'd never done anything of the sort.

After calling around and finding that nobody I knew had heard from Kevin, I contacted the local police to let them know about his disappearance. They opened an investigation into his whereabouts and asked me a battery of questions. I knew that Kevin would hate me for doing this if he was just off somewhere trying to have a bit of privacy, but given the circumstances, it was the only obvious course of action. I'd deal with his annoyance and frustration when that time came.

As I mentioned earlier, Kevin had spoken about taking his life since I first met him many years earlier. It wasn't something he ever talked about in an emotionally charged, melodramatic way, it was something he would bring up from time to time in calm conversation as a possibility he had long considered for himself. He was chronically ill, and was never shy about the fact that if nothing about his condition changed, one day he might choose to throw in the towel on this life. His will to live was immense, however, and these passing comments never felt like they would lead to anything. They felt like conversations about a very distant, hypothetical, and unlikely reality. With him now missing, however, and with his situation having recently reached a low point, it seemed like the most logical conclusion was that Kevin had actually done it. He had actually decided he was tired of the battle for his health, and chose to leave this life and body behind.

In the weeks after Kevin's disappearance, the grief, anguish, and guilt that I felt are difficult to describe. There was nothing else on my mind. One night, I was on the phone with my friend Erin, who was one of the only other people Kevin had been speaking with regularly before he went missing. She told me that during the entire previous day, she'd felt Kevin's presence. According to her, the sensation of his presence was incredibly strong, calming and beautiful.

"It just felt like him, Miles," she said. "I can't really describe it, but I know what I felt. It was Kevin, and he was everywhere. I could feel him in the wind, in the sunlight, in the atmosphere, and all through my body. And I just felt so much love from him. It was so beautiful!"

Coincidentally, Erin had lost her husband to suicide many years earlier, and explained to me that in the days after her husband's death, she had experienced the same profound sensation of his presence.

"I just know, Miles," she continued, "Kevin's actually gone now. He's dead. And he's okay. I just know."

I wasn't convinced. My mind thought of all sorts of alternative scenarios that could be taking place. Kevin could be cohabitating with a woman, on a trip, or any number of other possibilities. He could have had a secret life we never knew about that he quietly fled to. There was no doubt in my mind that he was clever enough to pull off such a feat.

As Erin finished explaining that she was no longer uncertain as to where Kevin was, I stared out the window of my pitch dark apartment at the night sky above downtown

Vancouver. As I thought about what she was saying and stared at the tops of buildings and the stars above them, a massive shooting star slowly streamed across the sky. I couldn't believe my eyes.

Seeing a shooting star at any time is special, but seeing one above a city's lights (not exactly ideal stargazing conditions), and in that particular moment, shook me. It felt like Kevin was winking at me, his ebullient, hyperactive and powerful light shining from the other side, nodding that indeed, he was no longer bound to his aching, tortured body here on earth. He was free, and he was bright.

To be honest, the same way that Erin 'just knew' Kevin had passed, at that moment, in my gut, there was no longer any hoping, or any question as to his fate. It wasn't something I could rationally explain, and it's something that wouldn't be confirmed until over a year later when his body was found and identified, but my heart felt that he'd left. And so after that conversation, I decided to grieve Kevin's departure as though I knew for certain that he had died, instead of remaining in the incredibly difficult place of not knowing indefinitely.

For the next month or so, I largely disconnected from the world to be with my feelings of confusion, grief, guilt and gratitude. Kevin was the most significant person in my life for the eight years leading up to this moment, and he'd suddenly left, forever, in a very intense way. I felt an aching sense of responsibility, given my closeness to him. I felt that I'd failed him as a friend. I felt confused about what it all meant. Where was he now? And how was he doing? I felt it was necessary to just be with all of this. Nothing else mattered.

One of the things that was very helpful at this time was an obscure meditation or prayer that Erin came across for mourning the dead. It involved setting aside a specific amount of time every morning and evening for the month after a loved one has died. During these allotted times, one is to meditate and pray on the transition of their loved one's soul. The intention is to send love and support to the soul as it makes its transition away from this life and into what lies beyond, cheering them on from earth, letting them know how much they are still loved here and how grateful we are for the blessings they brought to our lives while they were living with us. By sending all of this love and support, they might receive some comfort, strength and reassurance as they navigate a big transition. The goal is to help them, to cheer them on with love and praise.

This sounded like a good idea to me, and so I agreed to do it morning and evening for thirty minutes at a time. The tears of love and gratitude I cried for Kevin during these daily sessions may not have reached his soul or offered any comfort to it, but the healing they provided to my own heart was profound.

This prayer gave my grief and sadness a direction, a purpose that was life-affirming and constructive. I could tell Kevin all the things my heart wanted to, and I could do something with the love, sadness, confusion and reverence that at other times seemed to overwhelm me.

One other thing I found very helpful during this time was filling myself with perspectives on death and the afterlife. I went to the library on numerous occasions and filled my arms with nearly every book I found on grief, near-death experiences, past lives and various other subjects in this area. I read the works of well-known and celebrated authors like Elizabeth Kubler-Ross and Robert Monroe, but really took whatever I could get my hands on. I wanted to devour a wide range of experiences and wisdom others had accumulated and see if there were common threads that emerged concerning death and what lies beyond it, as a very innocent part of me simply wanted to understand where Kevin was now.

Of course, Kevin and I had discussed death countless times. I clearly remember him saying: "Death is a complete joke, Miles. The idea that we die with our bodies is totally absurd. Nobody dies! That's ridiculous, it's the biggest joke there is! It's more like waking up from a dream into a more real reality. Death isn't real."

I intellectually tended to agree with Kevin on this matter, but his conviction was far greater than mine. It was like he'd kept one foot in that other world, the soul level of reality, and so the idea of mortality was patently absurd to him. Although I liked the sound of that philosophically, actually having someone so close and important to me pass in such an intense way forced me to take a good long look at it all. The library was one of the places I turned to for answers.

Some days I read more than one book, soaking in another person's account of their near-death experience, past life regressions, or perspective from years of work in hospice care. I'd read a lot in my life, but never this much. My heart was ravenous for as much information on this subject as it could get. The more I read, the more certain universalities in the various perspectives began to emerge. And the more of these universalities I began to see, the more I could wrap my head around what just might be going on, what Kevin might be experiencing. Nothing could be certain, but my reading helped broaden the realm of what was possible in my mind.

There were several occasions during my prayer or meditation sessions when I vividly felt or saw Kevin, and many coincidences or synchronicities in the months after his passing which felt like they had his fingerprints all over them. Shortly after he went missing, I had to do a couple of days work that I'd previously agreed to as an extra on film sets. I needed the money at the time, but given how deep in grief I was it felt challenging to pull myself together and step out into the world. Fortunately, as an extra, very little was required of me. Most of the days were spent sitting around waiting for brief moments on set where I was used more or less as a silent prop. I brought some of the books I was reading along with me to the shoot and tried to make the best of the situation, which in the end actually turned out to be a good opportunity for me to get out of my bubble of isolation.

The first of these two days of work was on a wedding scene for a TV movie. During the shoot I wore a tux and sat with a bunch of other men and women in a wedding reception as the actors staged their drama before us. It wasn't until the middle of the day that I realized the male lead character, who was the groom in this wedding scene, was named Kevin. There was a big banner on the wall of the set that said something to the effect of "Congratulations Kevin and Jennifer!"

In the scene, Kevin and his bride, Jennifer, were taking their first dance after exchanging wedding vows, when suddenly the reception was interrupted by a gunshot. Kevin then fell to the ground, with a bleeding gunshot wound to his heart, and died in the arms of his beloved (who screamed "Kevin! Kevin! No!"). It's a mystery who shot and killed Kevin during that scene, though it is later revealed that it was the jealous sister of his bride (Jennifer) who fired the fatal gunshot.

I couldn't believe my eyes. All I had been thinking about for days was Kevin dying (and wondering to myself if Kevin was, in fact, dead), and now I was watching a scene of Kevin dying. What was even more striking, however, was that the woman Kevin had recently experienced such a bitter breakup and falling out with was named Jenny. I won't pretend to know what any of this meant, but it was certainly notable.

The second day of work was on a different production's set. This production was a superhero television show. The scene we were shooting was a funeral scene, with nothing notable other than the fact that once again, all I was thinking about was death, and that was what I saw acted out before me.

In the days and months that followed, I went through many waves of grief. I questioned my experience with Kevin as a whole, and wondered if there was something about our entire connection that had been fundamentally off. I wondered if everything I'd learned from him had been wrong. I looked very honestly and deeply at this, but one thing seemed absolutely certain: I'd learned how to feel my feelings and open my heart with Kevin's help. I'd begun to develop a relationship with my wounds and truth thanks to him, and nothing about that was a waste, misguided or done in vain. It felt like nothing could be more important, and so alongside any lingering confusion or questions that remained in me, I held a very solid recognition of the unbelievably valuable gifts I had received.

A year and a half after Kevin died, I was walking along a quiet, forested path in Stanley Park thinking about him, as I often do. On this particular morning, he came into my mind as I was thinking about planning for my future and making responsible financial choices. Kevin never gave much thought to these matters, living very much in the moment, and sometimes quite precariously so. I thought to myself: "Kevin neglected this part of his life so badly that he eventually took his own life, in part because of the drama it created for him."

Underneath this thought was the notion that Kevin's death had occurred in vain, and was the unfortunate result of blocks and challenges within himself he had failed to address or overcome in his life. Looking at his story from a certain angle, this could be considered a very reasonable thought to have. As it passed through my mind, however, I noticed that my energy felt extremely off - I felt ungrounded, twisted up inside and gross. In other words, it didn't feel like what I was thinking was in truth. It actually felt disturbingly disconnected from truth. It felt wrong.

Noticing this, I decided to try and look at Kevin's death from a different angle. I looked at it not as a tragic, untimely, morbid result of past mistakes, wrong choices and missed opportunities. I looked at it instead as though Kevin was done what he came here to do in this life. He had simply finished his sacred mission, and went back to the light from which he came. I imagined his light, or his soul, vacating his body and moving on, brilliantly shooting through space like the shooting star I'd seen one evening shortly after he died. His death, like his life, was not a tragedy, not an accident, not a failure. It was a divine transition, perfect in every way.

I let myself experience how sacred and beautiful that perspective felt. It felt heavenly. I was deeply moved by this, staring down at the forest path at my feet while I walked along and ruminated on it. When I eventually raised my eyes and looked ahead of myself, I saw a coyote walking towards me, a stone's throw away down the dirt path. This coyote must have raised its eyes at the same time as I did, as we seemed to notice one another and stop in our tracks simultaneously. Without expressing any alarm or worry, the graceful coyote turned around and sauntered away from me, silently slipping into the forest.

I'd only ever seen a coyote up close in the flesh once previously, and the timing of this encounter felt very notable. I've learned over the years to not try and attribute meaning to all of life's events (oftentimes, particularly for anxiety-prone individuals who might project their fears and insecurities onto every experience, it's better to not seek a deeper meaning to events at all, and just aim to live life with an open heart), but the intensity of what I'd just been thinking and feeling made this coyote's appearance stand out. I am somewhat aware of the mythology around coyote, in which he plays the role of the sacred trickster, bringing divine lessons to the world in ways that are humorous, malevolent, and not easily defined as either good or evil, existing somewhere beyond the limitations of simple, crude human understanding. Seeing a coyote in that moment, given what I'd been experiencing and letting in, felt significant.

Later that same day, a friend invited me to join her at a pub for a short visit. I accepted her invitation, and met her for a brief get together at an establishment named Stanley's Bar and Grill. As we got seated on the patio, I realized that I'd been to this place before: That wedding scene where I was an extra, while an actor playing 'Kevin' was shot and killed, was filmed inside this restaurant. It gave me shivers being back there, especially just hours after my process around Kevin's death.

Also worth noting is that there was an actual, real wedding ceremony taking place on the lawn just beside the patio this afternoon. It was quite a beautiful ceremony, and nobody was shot during it.

When I told my friend, Milota (who had also been friends with Kevin, and is extremely empathic herself), how I'd been to this restaurant before, and explained the circumstances under which that visit occurred, she shared that she had in fact just been talking about Kevin with someone immediately before coming to meet me.

She explained: "I was trying to look at things that Kevin could have done differently to heal his illness, and things he could be doing today if he was still here. But I kept on getting stopped while I was talking about it. The only thing that felt right or stayed open when I looked at it all was that Kevin actually died at the perfect time. He had shared his truth in a clear way to everyone, and had the experiences that served him most to have. He had a sacred purpose he'd fulfilled. I just arrived at a very clear place where it feels like there's no other way I can look at his death."

That I'd been brought back to this location, to witness another wedding, and hear Milota echo nearly the exact same dialogue I'd just had with myself, immediately after having had that dialogue (and encountering a coyote), certainly made me feel like a sacred trickster was arranging all of these things.

More importantly, it helped me acknowledge, at a deep level, that Kevin's life didn't truly *feel* like a mistake to me. His death didn't feel like a mistake, either. It all felt profoundly divine.

That I was one of the fortunate individuals to cross his path and be graced by his brilliance, wisdom, empathy and courage, is a blessing I will be forever grateful for, and have been forever changed by.

Chapter Twelve

A few months after Kevin disappeared, I got word that my Uncle Bob had died. I hadn't spoken to Uncle Bob (who was my father's oldest brother) in years, and frankly, I didn't think I would ever speak to him again. He wasn't someone I felt a great sense of kinship with. On the contrary, he was in many ways the embodiment of the inherited patterns I was learning to step out of. When I got the news of his passing, I felt no sense of loss, no desire to have shared any final words with him, no fondness for the good qualities he possessed. I felt resentment towards him, something I'd uncovered and explored a number of times over the previous several years. And while there were reasons behind my resentment, I had to admit to myself that my heart was completely closed while I was in it. I felt a sense of having been done wrong by a bad, unloving person, and a resulting anger that didn't feel clean, clear, or connected to the bigger truth. It felt like I was stuck in a wound, with my heart slammed shut, wanting to blame someone and make them wrong.

As I recognized all that was going on in me, I decided to try and explore the possibility of opening my heart in this situation - the possibility of opening my heart to Uncle Bob.

The mere thought of this made a part of me squirm - I'd never thought I would actually *want* to open my heart to Uncle Bob, but there was no hiding the fact that how I was relating to him felt awful. It felt disempowered, harsh and unkind.

I had done some emotional work around Uncle Bob several years earlier. Feelings around him had surfaced spontaneously on a couple of occasions, much to my surprise. I hadn't given him much thought over the years, and never considered him a person of great significance in my life. Upon closer inspection, however, I was mistaken.

When I was just beginning my journey of living in the woods, I'd asked Uncle Bob at one point to show me some of the backwoods skills he knew. Uncle Bob was an avid outdoorsman, a fisherman and a hunter, and was one of the only adults I knew that could pass practical knowledge in this area on to me. A part of me felt incredibly excited at the idea of him taking me out into the woods and sharing some of his wisdom.

On one occasion we made a plan to go on a fishing excursion together, but before that came to fruition, Uncle Bob backed out, and decided he wasn't interested in connecting in this way after all. It was as though he suddenly had a wall up, and was completely cut off from and disinterested in bonding or mentoring me in this realm. I was disappointed and hurt, because I never had experienced the kind of mentorship or connection that might have been possible through exploring the outdoors with an older man. From then on, I resented and lost respect for my Uncle. I was angry at him for not seeing and embracing a clear opportunity to support and teach his young nephew, who was clearly looking to him and asking for that. I honestly couldn't understand how he didn't jump at this opportunity, it had felt so sacred and good when we initially talked about it. Uncle Bob would instead probably be getting drunk at the bar with his buddies, as he often did, and a tender part of me that had wanted to feel supported by him was infuriated by that.

Sitting with my feelings of resentment, I decided to try and see Uncle Bob from a bigger perspective. Instead of looking at him through the eyes of an angry young man (whose feelings I'd already welcomed back into my awareness), I challenged myself to look at him as a soul, to see him as completely as I could, and find out if that might open my heart.

I closed my eyes, and began to remember everything I knew about Uncle Bob. The first thing that popped into my awareness was that his father (my paternal grandfather) had died suddenly in a workplace accident when Uncle Bob was a teenager. His father had been an avid woodsman himself, and I imagined Uncle Bob probably gained his lifelong passion for the outdoors through their early bonding together in that area. I imagined how sad and confused my Uncle Bob must have been to lose his father at that age. Uncle Bob was the oldest child of the family, so would surely have been wanting for support and guidance from elders. My sense is that he probably received very little of this in his grief. From what I remember hearing, his mother (my Granny), started living a somewhat unstable lifestyle in the wake of her husband's death. She remarried a few years later, but in the interim, the story was that she distracted herself with alcohol and going out with friends. I got the feeling that Uncle Bob was basically alone with a broken heart, at a time and in a family where feelings (and men's feelings in particular) weren't talked about, weren't honoured, and more often than not were drowned out with alcohol. Indeed, as far as I knew, Uncle Bob was raised in an environment of emotional disconnection, alcoholism or alcohol abuse, and harshness.

As I felt into all of this, I let myself go as deep into what he might have experienced as possible. I didn't want to just cerebrally think about this man's history, I wanted to feel it to my core. Before long I was crying.

Uncle Bob had a son who I never met. His name was Tommy, and from what I had been told, when Tommy was a child, Uncle Bob simply disconnected from him and his mother. I don't recall if he'd been married to Tommy's mother or not, but for some reason, Uncle Bob had just vanished from their lives. For as long as I knew him, Uncle Bob was married to my Auntie Joan, with whom he had a daughter, my cousin Selena. But Tommy was always an enigma to me, the son my Uncle Bob had abandoned.

As I continued feeling into this, something suddenly clicked, and I wondered if Uncle Bob abandoning Tommy was somehow related to the loss of his own father. Maybe since he'd had his initial father-son experience ruptured so traumatically, he couldn't bear to walk through that dynamic again, even with himself now in the parental role. I wondered, also, if him suddenly having a wall up with me as soon as I reached out in a way that could have led to a certain level of closeness and intimacy, was also related to his unprocessed wounds. I distinctly remember the bizarre energy Uncle Bob had when he told me he wanted to cancel our fishing expedition plans - he seemed incredibly distant, cold, meek and closed off from me. It was a stark contrast from his usual, gregarious self - it actually didn't feel like him. Upon reflection, it looked a lot like a person who was triggered, who had a wound that was activated and had taken hold of their awareness.

As these thoughts and observations flowed through me, I continued to try and really feel what this all might have been like for my Uncle Bob. I also let myself feel my disappointment in him, and then imagined how he might feel about himself in relation to some of the choices he had made. That was a sobering thought, as I suspect nobody would have felt more disappointment around some of his life choices than he himself.

Holding all of this, my heart opened to Uncle Bob. My eyes were filled with tears, and I felt deep compassion for this soul, who had been bruised, who had stumbled and blundered, and who also had been a joyous, warm, playful, and generous man through all of that. There was a reason I wanted to head into the woods with him, after all. He was fun, charismatic, strong, and boisterous. His good qualities were really good.

Suddenly, I could hold both of these realities together, the dark and light of Uncle Bob, and do so without a sense of resentment or anger. The part that had been hurt by him now had a context for who he was and how he had lived. I never thought I would even want to stretch myself into opening my heart to Uncle Bob, but it sure felt good to do so. Something shifted in a meaningful way after this process - a part of me that had been trapped in a sense of powerlessness and indignation was now free. It was no longer a little kid expecting something a flawed but beautiful person couldn't give him. It was grown now, and able to see the deeper truth and nuance of what had taken place. It saw the beauty and divinity of Uncle Bob.

In the wake of my Uncle Bob process, another unresolved matter began coming into my awareness: My Dad. I remember speaking to Daniel at the time, explaining how amazing it felt to be able to see my Uncle Bob in a new light, and for my heart to be loving and free in relation to him. When I honestly looked at my Dad, however, the same could not be said. The mere thought of him made me uncomfortable. It felt as though a young part of me was still trapped in a sense of betrayal, indignation and anger at him, and given what I'd just experienced around Uncle Bob, I wondered if it was time to look at things with my Dad a bit more deeply.

For a couple of weeks, I repeatedly tried to break through the way my heart was closed to my father. I did similar things to what I'd done with Uncle Bob, trying to put myself into my father's shoes, but for some reason it just wasn't working. My heart wouldn't budge. In retrospect, I think my heart was just more committed to keeping my Dad out, because there was more at stake with him, more vulnerability and more hurt.

It's probably worth noting that this was by no means the first time I'd done emotional work around my relationship with my father. Over the years, it was one of the most common recurring themes of my heart excavation. The amount of time I'd spent exploring, owning and expressing feelings of hurt and rejection related to my father was vast.

It felt very important to own the anger and sadness that I'd buried over the years. I'd come to understand that it isn't actually possible to forgive someone if you haven't let yourself fully own and experience how they hurt you in the first place. So my initial step was to own and acknowledge all of these difficult feelings. But after years of doing this, I could feel how my heart was still closed to my father. I could feel that a part of me was still stuck in the past, stuck in a power dynamic where I was small and angry. There was another step I needed to take, and I was trying, but it wasn't coming easily.

One afternoon I was out for a long walk in Stanley Park. It was early spring, and countless flowers were in bloom. I was listening to some beautiful music on my headphones, and once again trying to explore opening up my heart to my father.

This time, I really let myself go into the process. I decided to try and experience my father's whole life in my imagination and in my heart. I think the particular music I was listening to and the natural beauty I was surrounded by must have helped soften me a bit, because what had seemed impossible for weeks, suddenly opened up for me on this afternoon.

I imagined my Dad beginning his life as a toddler - an incredibly sensitive, innocent, curious and playful boy. His father had died in that tragic workplace accident when he was very young - somewhere between two and four years old. The same shock that rocked his teenage brother, Uncle Bob, hit my Dad at an incredibly vulnerable age. I imagined the confusion and overwhelm he would have felt as this tragedy struck his family. One of the pillars of his life was suddenly gone, and every older person around him was broken-hearted by this, but probably incapable of processing their feelings in a healthy way. His mother became distant, consumed by distractions (or, as I'd heard one of my uncles remark at one point, partying). His older brothers became more cruel, and began bullying and tormenting him. I felt my Dad's little heart being trampled. I felt his little nervous system being overwhelmed.

I imagined what it must have been like to not be able to talk to anyone about all that he was feeling. On the contrary, he would have received messages from those around him that he shouldn't talk about his feelings, and that expressing vulnerability was an invitation for ridicule or violence. I imagined what a horrific trap this would have felt like for his sensitive heart.

Again, this was not a purely cerebral exercise. I was using my imagination, but I was also equally using my empathy. I was trying to literally feel what he might have felt and how it would have shaped him, excusing whatever details I got wrong along the way. I continued feeling into who my father became, and the resentment he carried with him from his formative experiences.

I imagined him growing into manhood, his emotions never getting a chance to adequately breathe, evolve or be honoured as the duties of fatherhood consumed his energy and attention.

My arrival in his world had been unplanned - my parents told me many years earlier that I was the result of an accidental pregnancy - and I imagined the mixed reaction he may have had to this unforeseen responsibility at the time.

I saw his struggle to be a provider for our family. I saw how frustrating and difficult his experiences as a fledgling business owner with three young children and a marriage could be at times. I saw him go through disappointments, loss, and being taken advantage of. He was an incredibly sensitive man, and I watched how not dealing with his feelings in a healthy way could turn him into the brooding, frustrated, closed-hearted person I reacted so strongly against. I saw how his discomfort with his own vulnerability made him bully and judge the vulnerability of others. I watched him cover his insecurity with a brittle armour, an awkwardness, unnaturalness and superficial way of relating to others.

As I witnessed all of this and more, I noticed something very exciting: I wasn't reacting with anger or disgust to any of it. I was actually nodding my head, as a fellow card-carrying member of the emotionally convoluted, sensitive asshole club. Every one of the patterns I was feeling and observing in my father was something I was fully guilty of living out myself. In fact, I was pretty sure that my personal versions of all of these patterns were much more mean, harsh and intense than his.

And, as I looked back to the beginning of my father's life and the genesis of these patterns, he seemed very innocent. I couldn't imagine who I might have become had I been raised in an environment of such harshness, dysfunction and loss. As tears streamed down my face, I saw what a unique challenge his life experiences had been. I also saw the goodness of him that had persevered and shined through all of that. I felt what a gift his kindness and sensitivity had been for me as a child. He was a very loving, caring man, capable of great joy, compassion and playfulness. From where I was looking, I saw these parts of him with a deep sense of awe and gratitude.

Finally, my heart was open. I was able to look at my Dad from a bigger perspective, beyond the sense of hurt and smallness I had been stuck in for so long. I was able to look at him not as a flawed person who couldn't give me something I wanted, but as a peer, as another soul on a journey, moving through this life with their sacred gifts and their sacred wounds.

While I have by no means arrived at an endpoint in this process, the heart opening I experienced that day was very significant. It was actually surprisingly easy to open my heart to my Dad, once I got into it. In the same way that my heart is pretty soft and mushy directly beneath its unsophisticated defences, my Dad felt like a pretty easy guy to understand and to love. All it took was being willing to feel into my hurt, and show it a bigger picture. But sometimes things that are very simple technically, are completely dumbfounding when raw emotion, vulnerability, and a hurt heart are involved.

A couple of years before he died, Kevin and I were having a conversation on the phone when he began processing a part of my energy. He explained to me that he'd taken on some of my unprocessed emotion, and needed to clear it out of himself to get centred. As he did this, he drifted into an exploration of my energy and wounds overall, intuitively studying and surveying the landscape of my being, while giving me a play-by-play commentary on everything he was seeing. At one point, he dove into the most wounded, twisted, and sinister part of my consciousness, and made some rather sobering observations.

"Miles," he said, "all I see in you is darkness. When I look deep, I honestly don't see any light in you whatsoever. I've never experienced this with anyone before, and I know it must sound awful and be hard to hear, but I literally can't find any light anywhere in you. All I see is twisted, vicious, malevolent energy. It's literally all there is when I go beneath the surface. This is unbelievable!"

Kevin continued his intuitive exploration as I sat and listened in a state of horror. I wondered to myself: Am I simply evil to the core? Do I lack the basic spark of goodness that all other humans contain? Kevin couldn't find any light whatsoever within me - this was bad news. During this conversation, a very innocent part of me, a part that put Kevin in a position of great trust and authority, completely believed that I may be fundamentally evil, some kind of demonic shadow being, it so heavily valued Kevin's perspective (and so easily relinquished its sense of fundamental goodness).

After about five minutes or so of searching, Kevin made a discovery: "Oh, there it is," he said. "Yep, I see some light now. Wow, okay, that was confusing for a second."

Having found some light and goodness in my energy, he quickly dropped the theory that I was a strange kind of cursed entity. During the moments when he was uncertain about all of this, however, my own sense of innate decency and goodness pretty much collapsed.

Looking back, I think this whole experience was funny, and emblematic of something clearly askew in how I related to Kevin (and people in general). The fact that Kevin could get so affected by one wounded part of me that he questioned my essential goodness as a soul was one thing (I actually think it was amazing that he was so honest about his process, and shared everything he was experiencing in the moment), but more noteworthy than that was me totally hanging onto his every word, and losing my basic sense of self-worth as a result.

That I could be so easily nudged by another's whims into questioning my essential goodness, at the deepest possible level, and wonder if all there was to me was rotten evil, was incredible.

It later occurred to me that this was something I had done throughout my whole life: I had let the limited perceptions of others determine my sense of self, and disconnect me from a sense of my innate sanctity. I'd let other people's passing comments and closed hearts (and my interpretations of them) close my heart.

There is a risk in any teacher-student relationship that the student will give their power away, that they will lose their sense of autonomous wisdom and direction. As the experience I just related demonstrates, there were times when this undeniably happened with myself and Kevin. But this was a pattern of mine that predated our connection by many years.

Earlier in this book, I shared an experience of making contact with myself as a fetus - witnessing a prenatal version of me take on the idea that he was a burden, that he was a mistake and somehow fundamentally flawed. Whether what I saw during that experience was completely historically real or not, it is true that at an early age, I developed a very unloving and unkind view of myself, based on things I felt, interpreted, and misinterpreted from those around me. I accepted these limited perceptions of myself as reality, and disowned my own sense of divine goodness when it wasn't clearly held and mirrored back to me.

What a strange gift, then, to get to experience a version of this dynamic again with a man who could teach me how to see exactly what was going on. Kevin showed me how to open and access my heart and develop a relationship to truth in ways I couldn't even imagine before we met. Because of his brilliance, however, I also put him on a pedestal, and developed a very diminished sense of myself, as well as a deep feeling of unworthiness, in relation to him. This diminished sense of self, it should be noted, had nothing to do with the wisdom of my open heart or my truth. It was part of a mental script that required me to close my heart and disconnect from truth before it could be entertained or believed.

One of the things I've been learning, is that to maintain an open heart, one needs to remain connected to their innate sense of goodness and sanctity *even when the people and world around them cannot or do not appear to clearly reflect that* - even when people and the world question, challenge or actively contradict it. There were times in my past when family, friends, and strangers did not reflect my innate goodness back to me in a clear way. There are often times when the world itself doesn't appear to reflect it at all. And my understanding is, that's the whole point. That's one of the most brilliant parts of life here, and is actually something that helps our hearts evolve in their capacity to love. We are here to learn to love bravely, to love unconditionally, and in an environment that can appear at times to be devoid of love, truth, and empathy, to maintain our faith and devotion to them. We are here to open our hearts, even when others seem to be closed, and let the world respond.

Acknowledgements

This book would not have been possible were it not for the wisdom, grace and influence of a number of extraordinary people that I have been blessed to have as friends and teachers over the past decade. First, I'd like to thank Daniel Dowker, a friend across the ages, for the role you have played in my life and in my growth as a soul, and also for the brilliant, invaluable editorial feedback you gave me during the final stages of writing and refining this book, as well as your amazing cover concept. Your profound, empathic heart and far-reaching wisdom have been sources of incredible insight and richness for me. You were pivotal in all of this, thank you.

I would also like to thank Milota Weinwurm, another friend across many chapters of this life, whose presence in my world has been an extraordinary blessing. Your incredible sensitivity, vision, pure heart and grace are beautiful gifts that I've been unbelievably fortunate to have in my world. Thank you for your encouragement and your energetic observations of the early manuscript of this book.

Your wisdom and clear, empathic vision helped steer me, and this book, in a truer and stronger direction. Thank you for being in my life.

A big thank you also to Erin Webster, whose presence during the part of this journey where Kevin departed was incredibly nurturing and supportive. Your wide-open, loving heart, depth of understanding and authentic kindness have been incredibly nourishing elements in my world. Thank you for offering your impressions of the manuscript for this book and helping me to see some important places where it could be cleaned up. Thank you also for your loving encouragement and support.

And last, but certainly not least, an enormous thank you to Kevin Hodgson. Just how much richer and more beautiful my life and this world are because of you, I cannot imagine even trying to capture in words. You changed everything for me, forever, and I cannot thank you enough. Your courage, vision, honesty and connection to truth were forces of nature - they changed the course of so many people's lives and continue to do so. The brilliance you brought into this world was a thing of such sophistication, elegance, complexity and grace, that I continue to scratch my head and marvel in awe at it, as I would before any other sacred force of nature. Thank you Kevin, from the bottom of my heart. I love and appreciate you so much, and there are a lot of others here that do, too. Whatever you're up to now, I hope you can feel some of that love and appreciation. It's massive.

From The Author

Thank you so much for reading this book. If you've enjoyed what you have found in these pages and would like to help it reach the hands of others, please consider giving it a review on Amazon. Doing so will not only make me incredibly grateful, but will also tangibly help spread this book's reach across the world.

If you'd like to see what I'm up to at the moment, visit milesolsen.com, where you'll find what I'm currently working on and sharing. Again, thank you for reading - it's an honour to have these words and this story welcomed into your world.

About The Author

Miles Olsen is an author whose honest and direct storytelling takes readers on a deep exploration of empathy and vulnerability. His work brings a joyful, raw, and penetrating light to the realm of emotional and empathic development.

Made in the USA
Las Vegas, NV
28 November 2023

81626546R00132